THE
POWER
of the
DECREE

THE
POWER
of the
DECREE

RELEASING THE AUTHORITY
OF GOD'S WORD
THROUGH DECLARATION

PATRICIA KING

Chosen

a division of Baker Publishing Group
Minneapolis, Minnesota

Published by Chosen Books
Minneapolis, Minnesota
ChosenBooks.com

Chosen Books is a division of
Baker Publishing Group, Grand Rapids, Michigan

Printed in the United States of America

Library of Congress Cataloging–in–Publication Data
Names: King, Patricia, author.
Title: The power of the decree: releasing the authority of God's word through declaration
/ Patricia King.
Description: Bloomington, Minnesota: Chosen Books, [2020]
Identifiers: LCCN 2019057456 | ISBN 9780800799694 (trade paperback) | ISBN
9781493424818 (ebook)
Subjects: LCSH: Christian life–Biblical teaching. | Bible–Evidences, authority, etc. | Bible–
Use. | Word of God (Christian theology)
Classification: LCC BS680.C47 K57 2020 | DDC 248.4/6–dc23
LC record available at https://lccn.loc.gov/2019057456

In some cases, the names and identifying details of certain individuals have been changed to protect their privacy.

Cover design by Rob Williams, InsideOutCreativeArts

Baker Publishing Group publications use paper produced from sustainable forestry practices and postconsumer waste whenever possible.

24 25 26 27 28 29 30   9 8 7 6 5 4 3

Contents

Contents

Foreword

The words we speak are powerful. They can wound and they can heal. They can affirm and they can accuse. How much more powerful do our words become when we confess the truths of God! A decree is an official order issued by a legal authority. A decree is taking God's words and speaking them out. A decree from our lips can be loaded with life, restoring the fallen and reviving the forsaken.

We have been given the authority from Jesus to speak decrees into our realms of influence, and as we do, we begin to create the will of God in our lives in the spiritual realm. I know without any doubt that speaking decrees over our lives and families can change our circumstances.

I once faced a horrible situation that I know was turned around when I made a decree from my mouth. Let me tell you about it.

My wife, Candice, and I were serving Christ as missionaries in the rainforest of Panama, living near the border of Colombia. The jungle surrounded us with all its dangers. One day our precious daughter was playing near the river with her friends, when suddenly one of the world's longest pit vipers, known as the bushmaster, latched onto her ankle. The venom of this pit viper is deadly. More than one person has died in the jungle from a bite from the bushmaster. The effects of the venom of this snake are many: swelling, throbbing pain and internal bleeding.

I carried our daughter into our hut and immediately began to pray, hard! I pleaded, I begged God to heal her, I wept, I sought God's healing power and asked heaven to spare her. But here is what turned it all around: I made a decree.

I spoke over her that we were sent by God to the jungle to win people to Christ, not bury a loved one. "You will live and not die!" I decreed heaven's power and healing grace over her life.

Then I felt the shift in the atmosphere all around us. I knew God was going to answer my prayer of decree.

Yes, you know the end of this story. She eventually got better and was healed. Today there is no sign of that poisonous snakebite in her life, for God worked a miracle.

How many miracles are waiting for our heavenly decrees? There are times we must push aside our fears and doubts and simply declare God's Word over our difficulties. Some might ask, "What is our authority to make a decree?" It is the name of Jesus. Everything must bow before the name of Jesus. It is the one and only name that has power on earth, in heaven and in hell.

You can use the name of Jesus as though He Himself, with all His authority, is standing beside you (see 1 Corinthians 6:17). King Jesus has given you the authority and power over demons, and you have the right to ask the Father for victory in His name (see Luke 10:19). John 14:13–14 (TPT) gives us one of the major weapons from the Throne Room—the name of Jesus:

> "For I will do whatever you ask me to do when you ask me in my name. And that is how the Son will show what the Father is really

like and bring glory to him. Ask me anything in my name, and I will do it for you!"

Use the name or names of Jesus in your decrees and watch heaven move on your behalf.

You hold in your hands a book written by an experienced, powerful servant of Christ. In *The Power of the Decree*, Patricia King takes us on a journey into the depths of God's authority and power that He means to operate in your life. You will read this and get excited. You will begin to speak life-giving words that will impact everything around you. You will see your family change, even your future change, by making decrees over what lies before you. Based solidly on Scripture and filled with practical information, this book may be the most effective book you have ever read to transform the world around you. Read it thoroughly and underline those statements that reverberate in your soul. Get ready for the booster rocket of *The Power of the Decree* to take you higher into the ways of God. You will be glad you chose this book.

Brian Simmons
The Passion Translation Project
www.passionandfire.com

PART ONE

THE
POWER
of the
DECREE

one

That Settles It!

Life is filled with challenges; you might be facing some right now. Perhaps you need a breakthrough in your finances, health, relationships or spiritual growth. You may have attempted to secure your breakthrough by hoping, praying, worshiping and remaining in healthy Christian fellowship, yet the adverse circumstances remain. The "mountain" has not yet moved.

I know exactly how that feels, as I have experienced similar frustrations. But God has given me a powerful solution and, in this book, I want to reveal to you the greatest Spirit-inspired key God has given me for sustained victory and breakthrough in life. Understanding this vital key and using it effectively has set me on a solid foundation, and I am convinced it will help you too. This key can powerfully transform your life, and I am excited to share it with you!

I was in a very broken and emotionally unstable place prior to receiving the Lord as my personal Savior. The night I invited Him into my heart was a transformational turning point for me.

Internally I knew I was a different person—a new creation—and yet so many circumstances remained in upheaval even as I prayed and believed.

Then my life was forever changed when I heard Dr. Oral Roberts preach a powerful sermon in which he emphatically and repeatedly declared, *"God said it. I believe it. That settles it!"* Those faith-infused declarations entered my heart that day and produced a fiery passion for the life-giving Word of God that continues to burn in me to this very hour.

Following this significant revelation, it became my practice to seek the Lord daily concerning the life situations that I was facing. I invited Him to give me insight and understanding into specific challenges, desires and longings. Waiting on Him in prayer, I searched the Scriptures. I found that, consistently and faithfully, the Holy Spirit would reveal God's will, perspective and promises through His Word.

Once I understood His will and ways concerning a situation, I learned to stand on His Word and "settle it." No matter what the circumstances were, I allowed the Word to be my plumb line and committed myself to that truth. By faith, I commanded everything to come into alignment with the Word, whether or not my current circumstances looked like it. And continuously, I began to witness answers to prayer, amazing breakthroughs and anointed empowerments that produced fruitfulness and success in God-appointed endeavors. Faith was cultivated in me as I believed what God said and determined to settle any issue in life according to His Word and its power to transform and create.

A few years into my walk with the Lord, my husband and I, along with our two young children, engaged in an evangelism/missions training program. This training organization depended on God for everything—the example they set was wonderful. They taught us to wait on God in prayer in deeper ways than we had understood previously, and we gained a Holy-Spirit-directed burden for the nations. We watched God answer prayers over and over.

This organization's emphasis was not so much on the Word (although they honored the Word), but rather on worship, intercession and character alignment. While all of these things are important and valuable, I found during my time in the program that my personal focus on and my commitment to the Word waned. It was no longer simply: "God said it. I believe it. That settles it!" As participants in the program, we sat through numerous sessions that emphasized Christian disciplines; we learned how to please God and gained insights on how we might have displeased Him. I began to buy into various distorted perspectives as to why God would not always fulfill His Word, and most of these perspectives were rooted in a belief that human failure caused His displeasure.

As a result, I found myself no longer focused on what the Word said about me as a beloved child of God, but rather on what my behavior and choices communicated. I so wanted to please God, and I began to strive to accomplish a level of behavioral acceptance in His sight. Although I was seeking Him with all my heart and we had left everything to follow Him, I still felt unworthy and often self-condemned. I always felt I was missing the mark, although I tried with everything in me to please Him. Having lost my confidence in His undeserved favor and unconditional love for me, I found it difficult to believe He would answer my prayers. In no way am I suggesting that our instructors were teaching error, but in that season of my life I was surely ensnared through my interpretation and application of their instruction.

James 1:23–25 teaches us that the Word is like a mirror and we are to see ourselves in the light of the perfect law of liberty.

When we walk away from the truth of the Word, we will forget who we are in Christ, and circumstances will then present to us a distorted image. That is exactly what happened to me. I felt that I was not pleasing to God because I could not perform well enough, even though the Word clearly declared that I was accepted in the Beloved (see Ephesians 1:6).

My acceptance in Him is based not on what I do but rather on what Christ accomplished for me two thousand years ago through His finished work on the cross. God said it. I should have believed it, and that should have settled it. But I had lost my focus. I was gazing on all my shortcomings and I had lost sight of the truth. It was a downhill slide for me—I lost my rest in Christ and experienced religious striving and self-condemnation.

Around that same time, an emphasis of biblical faith teaching emerged in the Body of Christ. This teaching encouraged believers to stand firmly in faith on the Word of God and not to allow themselves to be moved by circumstances. If God said it, it was true. This emerging movement had an emphasis on living the abundant life promised by Jesus (see John 10:10). Followers were taught to believe God's Word and to receive His promises with unwavering faith.

After attending one of their meetings, listening to the faith-infused teaching and examining the Scriptures carefully, my simple faith was restored. It was as though a veil had been removed from my understanding and it became clear once again: If God said it, I believe it. And that settles it. Oh, how wonderful to enjoy that simple childlike faith once again!

It is important to exalt God and His uncompromised Word in an hour when "darkness is covering the earth and gross darkness the people" (see Isaiah 60:2 KJV). We must honor and believe the Word. We must humbly align ourselves with the uncompromised, all-authoritative, all-powerful Word of God.

Living by Faith

It was in this season of freshly awakened faith in God's Word that the Lord called my husband, Ron, and me to leave our secular careers and serve Him full-time in missions and evangelism. The Lord invited us to live by faith with no visible means of financial support, and during that time He further instructed us to bring our needs before Him only and not to share them with others. Both Ron and I were excited for the opportunity to honor God in this way. In our evangelism/missions training program, we had seen God move in powerful provisional miracles on behalf of the missionaries serving in that organization, so we were looking forward to seeing Him move in our lives in similar ways. We gave God our hearty "yes" and we began the journey. Knowing that He is truly worthy, we laid everything on the altar for His glory and purposes.

We began our journey by studying the provisional Scriptures from Genesis to Revelation. We discovered that God always provided in abundance for His people who believed in Him. Lack was never on His agenda—this was absolutely clear in our study of the Scriptures. We proceeded to write out the verses that promised His unfailing provision and declared, "God said it. We believe it. That settles it!"

Well, declaring it was the easy part. We had no idea that we were about to face excruciating and painful realms of testing over the next five years as we committed to believing His Word *only*. Two things were to be tested:

1. Our "yes" to the calling of God
2. Our belief in His Word in the face of all contrary circumstances

Literally, all hell broke loose against us. It felt to us as though the devil had assigned every demon of lack and poverty in the universe against us. It was truly a painful time, and we had to find our faith in the midst of it. We continually returned to the Scriptures. We read them, prayed them, sang them and meditated on them. Those precious verses were God's promises to us. He said it, we believed it . . . and that should settle it. *But*—oh, the pain and the discouragement of believing His Word with all our hearts and not seeing an immediate manifestation of its truth.

We had given God our "yes," so there was no turning back. We had no Plan B. We continued to believe, but the provision was definitely invisible. We literally had to *believe* for food to appear on the table when there was no food to be found in the house. We had to believe for fuel when the gas tank was completely empty. It was discouraging to see our children in need during this season of testing. However, as a family we continued to honor the Word. We believed it and we obeyed it. We continued to tithe, give and sow as the Word instructs us, even when there was very little.

During this time Ron lost hope for a brief time and he fell into a depression. My husband is a very stable man, faithful, loving, hardworking and responsible. He is a gift from God to me . . . a rock. It broke my heart to see him so deeply affected. Once for two days he had a hard time getting out of bed due to the discouragement. I went into prayer and right away the Lord spoke to my heart, questioning me: "Do you believe I am Ron's Deliverer? Do you believe that I have a promise of victory and breakthrough for him?" My answer was a hearty "yes," and then I knew exactly what to do: Search the Scriptures! What does God say?

I discovered hope as I searched the Word and wrote out a full page of Scriptures that promised Ron victory over his sadness and over his perceived defeat as a provider for the family. The

Holy Spirit further instructed me—and this was big—to write out the Scriptures in the form of a decree from God's heart so that my husband could declare them as his very own personalized truth. For example, in John 8:36, Jesus said, "So if the Son makes you free, you will be free indeed." From that verse, I composed a written scriptural decree for Ron to proclaim: "The Son has made me free and therefore I am free indeed." I did the same with Scriptures such as 2 Corinthians 2:14, writing, "God always leads me in His triumph," and Romans 8:37—"In all these things I overwhelmingly conquer through Christ who loves me."

I prepared a full page of scriptural decrees for him to declare. However, in his depressed state, he was not at all motivated to declare them. He just wanted to sleep. So I became a little assertive and said, "I will decree them with you, but you *will* decree them!" He sat up in bed and barely whispered them. I honestly could not detect even a speck of faith as he read them through that first time. When he finished, he rolled over in bed, intending to go back to sleep. I lovingly fought him on that, saying, "No, you will continue to read these until you believe them and receive them." I then walked him through the second round and the third.

By the third time through, he was already brighter and ready to get out of bed. The Word is powerful! I informed him that we would declare these Scriptures again at least five times that day. In each of the five sessions, we proclaimed the decrees three times. The depression and hopelessness left in that one day of decrees and did not return. God had said it. We had believed it. And that had settled it!

I was thrilled at the breakthrough God gave us through the act of decreeing the truth. I later included that initial decree for victory in a book of decrees I wrote, and I have included it in a specific chapter on the subject later in this book. That initial decree created back in the 1980s—based on the Word of God written thousands of years ago—is still producing glorious outcomes in people's lives. The Word never gets old or ineffective.

The Scripture teaches that God's Word does not return void but accomplishes everything it is sent to do: "So will My word be which goes forth from My mouth; it will not return to Me empty, without accomplishing what I desire, and without succeeding in the matter for which I sent it" (Isaiah 55:11).

At the same time our oldest son, who was in the second grade, was facing a challenge in his academic studies. He lost his confidence as a result, and he was very discouraged. I realized it was becoming dangerous when I heard him saying things like, "I'm stupid. I can't do anything right." He was so young, and I was concerned. Having seen Ron achieve his great breakthrough through decreeing the Word, I decided to do the same for my son. I prepared decrees based on the Word of God that were written in a way that his young mind would be able to receive and apply. Instead of writing out the decrees for him, I recorded them on a tape recorder. I called it his "nighty-night tape." In it, I proclaimed decrees such as:

> *Jesus will strengthen you in all you do at school and at play.*
>
> *Like Daniel, you are smart in all wisdom, full of understanding and knowledge.*
>
> *You are God's own child—deeply loved and cherished.*
>
> *You are filled with wisdom and understanding in the knowledge of Christ.*
>
> *You have confidence in God and it gives you great reward.*
>
> *You are highly favored. Everyone loves you. God's favor protects you.*

God's face shines upon you with pleasure.
Your memory is blessed.
You are a champion in Jesus.
God's peace fills you. . . .

The decree recording was a full hour. Every night, he went to sleep with it on, and it continued to play as he slept. Within a very short time he gained confidence and his grades improved.

Psalm 119:130 teaches that the entrance of God's words brings light. When you decree the Word of God into someone's life or into a situation they (or you) are facing, it will not only establish that person or situation in truth but will cause light to expel darkness.

The decree of God's Word established my husband in confidence again and expelled the darkness of the depression by which he had been attacked. The decree of God's Word established my young son in renewed hope and vision and expelled the darkness of discouragement, self-condemnation and academic weakness.

Our family faced many battles in that season, but every day during the five-year period of testing, I intentionally reminded myself: "God said it. I believe it. That settles it!"

As I was learning about the power of decrees, a couple Ron and I were close to were experiencing severe marriage problems and were at the point of filing for legal separation and divorce. I made up a page of Scripture decrees that I proclaimed faithfully over their marriage in my prayer time. In a very short period, their marriage was healed, and they were enjoying a fresh, sweet love for each other. They continued to live happily until the husband's passing over thirty years later. The Word had gone to work. It did not return void but accomplished what it was sent to do.

God cares about everything that pertains to us—even things that seem small and insignificant. After that five-year season of testing, we started to minister among the poor in Tijuana, Mexico, which necessitated frequent trips from Vancouver, Canada, where we lived, to our mission field. We always ventured out in faith, as faith in God's Word alone was our only stable currency and promise of provision.

One time, as I was driving down to Tijuana with one of my prayer team members, our vehicle blew a tire on an isolated patch of highway in California. We pulled over to the side of the road and discovered that our spare was deflated—and neither one of us was very efficient with mechanical issues. We were stuck. We began to praise God. I remember looking at the tire and decreeing, "In the name of Jesus, you are repaired and filled with air." I repeated it over and over and soon began to laugh. It seemed a little ridiculous to be speaking to a tire. I continued to decree and laugh.

After about ten minutes or so, someone pulled up and asked us if we needed help. We explained what had happened. He kindly and enthusiastically said, "I surely believe I can help you." He went into the back of his truck and pulled out a brand-new tire—the exact size we needed! He changed the tire and we were ready to go. When I turned around to thank him, he was nowhere to be found and neither was his truck. We assumed it must have been an angel because we had no natural explanation. We will never know for sure whether or not he was an angel, but we do know for sure that the decree worked!

Over the many years that followed I exercised the power of decrees based on the Scriptures both in larger issues and smaller issues in life. I watched God faithfully move in response to the command of His own Word. Decreeing His Word brought forth results of peace, love, wisdom, healing, freedom and prosperity.

God desires all His people to live in His divine order and blessings. His Word is our plumb line, and decreeing it establishes His will and purpose in and through our lives. You and I were created to decree His Word.

In the following chapters, I will teach you how to discern the specific passage of Scripture that applies to your situation, how to stand in the presence of the Lord to hear the affirmation of His authoritative decrees and how to declare the decrees with confidence concerning anything in life you might face. My desire is for you to become skilled in the execution of God's will through decrees. I am confident that you will find decrees a God-given tool that you cannot live without. Every area of your life can flourish through decrees. Everything can align with God's will and His abundance. God says it. You can believe it. And that will settle it.

Testimonies from Those Who Decree the Word

God opened doors of favor for me

I love decrees! I was brand-new to being a professional photographer and I began to decree every morning that I would be the nation's leading political photographer and influence government officials with the Gospel of Jesus. Since making these decrees, I have had the opportunity to photograph presidents of the United States and many elected officials. Get the Word of the Lord and begin to decree it every day! What is finished in heaven will begin to manifest in your life before you know it.

—*Jonathan Williams*

Land healed by decrees

In 2009 my husband and I had an opportunity to purchase a commercial building and open an automotive dealership. It was a former gas station and the ground had been contaminated due to the under-ground gas tanks leaking into the environment for years.

So we decided to believe God to heal the land and began to walk the dealership lot and decree, "We call this land healed in the name of Jesus"; "We decree that all environmental poison will evaporate and the land will be clean." We also decreed a new name over the land, calling it "blessed" and "highly favored."

The environmental people from the government had been drill-ing bore holes and testing the soil every six months from the time we arrived due to the seriousness of the poison in the ground. We were told to expect this for a lifetime, and the big oil company who had built the gas station had signed a contract to be responsible for a lifetime of environmental cleanup.

But seven years after we started decreeing, they were able to stop testing because the bore holes were now coming back totally clean.

We eventually received a certificate from the government declar-ing that the land was now clean and was being taken off the official contaminated list.

Two years later we sold the property, and it had gone up so much in value that we were able to pursue some Kingdom dreams we have had for years!

—*Wendy Peter*

Establishing presence in first ministry office and studio

When we were establishing our ministry's new offices and studio, the Lord gave us a dozen Scriptures to decree over the land and building He had blessed us with. We faithfully decreed the scriptural promises of His presence, power, glory and blessings every day. We also wrote them on stakes and drove those declared promises into the ground of the new property. When we held our very first meeting in the new building, the manifest presence of God was so strong that everyone in attendance ended up on their faces overwhelmed by the tangible reality of our awesome and faithful God.

—*Robert Hotchkin*

Decrees gave us breakthrough in our marriage

Decreeing the Word of God brought the breakthrough we were needing. My husband and I walked into a tough season in our marriage and our relationship. God reminded me of the Scriptures that He gave us over our marriage and led me to other promises in His Word. By decreeing His Word continuously, we were able to move from defeat over our circumstances to victory! Our marriage is thriving because we chose to agree with God.

—Mari Maynard

Our financial breakthrough came as a result of decrees

During a season of financial challenge due to health issues in our family, the Lord highlighted Philippians 4:19 to me in *The Message* version:

> You can be sure that God will take care of everything you need, his generosity exceeding even yours in the glory that pours from Jesus. (Philippians 4:19 MSG)

I wrote this Scripture out and kept it taped to the window above my kitchen sink, renewing my faith as I often decreed it, sometimes several times each day. We saw God's hand at work in miraculous ways, with our bills always being supernaturally met each month, and we even had a special circumstance arise where we needed an additional $4,000 to pay a special tax bill, and within a one-week span, money came in from three unexpected sources and even that additional bill was met!

I am a firm believer in regularly decreeing Scripture and standing in faith on what the Word says!

—Lorrie Myers

90 percent of my medical bill waived

I was needing a creative financial breakthrough due to an unexpected medical emergency for one of my children. I held on to the promise that God is my provider. I remember not feeling defeated, but rather peace after getting off the phone with the medical insurance company that I was responsible to for this sizable debt. In that moment, I began to decree promises from the Word of God into that mountain of debt and into my finances. Within two weeks, I received a phone call from the medical provider that said they were looking at my situation and that they were going to waive over 90 percent of the amount owed. I LOVE decrees!!

—*Jamie Suiter*

From weeping to decreeing

A number of years ago I found myself crying over one of my children who was making unhealthy choices that were causing strain in our relationship. The Holy Spirit spoke to me and told me to stop weeping and to begin decreeing in my "secret place" the destiny call over my child's life that He had revealed in early childhood. I decreed it all by using Scriptures that confirmed the revealed call. It was only a few weeks when I realized that the atmosphere had shifted. Doors for conversations began to open and our relationship made a huge shift. As the years have passed, I continue to decree rather than weep. I have learned to trust God, and I see my child's huge God-ordained future unfolding. My burden is light as I rejoice in what He has done, is doing and continues to do. There is power in aligning with the Kingdom of heaven, and learning to decree made all the difference!

—*Ruth Hendrickson*

Sent the Word to heal

While ministering at a crusade in Nigeria, I gave a word of knowledge about someone who had spent all the money she had looking for a cure, but yet was not cured, and that the Lord was going to heal her. A breast cancer patient came forward for prayers. I decreed God's Word of healing over her body. Shortly afterwards she went for another biopsy and they could not find any cancer in her breast tissues. She was completely healed, with medical documentation.

—*Ella Onakoya*

QUESTIONS TO PONDER

1. What areas of your life currently need to be "settled" according to God's Word?

   _____

   _____

   _____

2. Do you believe that God wants you to have breakthrough in these areas? (If not, why not?)

   _____

   _____

   _____

3. Are you ready and willing to position yourself in God to "settle" these areas? Write a statement of commitment and date it.

   _____

   _____

   _____

two

Word: Confess, Proclaim or Decree?

At this point you might be excited about making decrees and dreaming about the possible effects of decrees on your life, but what exactly does it mean to decree and how is it different from confessing or proclaiming? Let's examine some definitions of each of these.

"Confess" Defined

When you confess, you are admitting or testifying. In the New Testament, the original Greek word for confess is *homologeō*, meaning to confess or acknowledge; to state personal belief.*
Here is the word as used in the familiar passage from the book of Romans: "If you *confess* with your mouth Jesus as Lord, and believe in your heart that God raised Him from the dead, you will be saved" (Romans 10:9, emphasis added).

*Strong's Concordance #3670.

I remember the night I asked Jesus to come into my heart. It was such a beautiful moment! I was so filled with His love that I wanted everyone in the whole world to know Him. The next morning, I met with my neighbors, testifying what had happened to me the night before and giving them an opportunity to know Christ, too. Later I contacted my close friends in order to confess my newfound faith in Christ and offer them an invitation to receive Him.

When you testify, you are making confession of what you believe.

Often confession is done privately, but it can also be public. At public baptisms, candidates confess their faith before witnesses prior to being immersed in the water. Sometimes people are called to confess in court on a witness stand; they testify under oath. At other times individuals will confess their sins as described in Scripture: "If we confess our sins, He is faithful and just to forgive us our sins, and to cleanse us from all unrighteousness" (1 John 1:9 NKJV).

A confession is powerful, but it is not the same as a decree.

"Proclaim" Defined

To proclaim means to announce something officially or publicly. In the Old Testament, the Hebrew root word is *qara'*, meaning to call out, recite, read, cry out.* When the Spirit of the Lord is upon us, we can bring anointed proclamations of the truth—official, public communications. We see an example of this word used by Isaiah:

> The Spirit of the Lord GOD is upon me, because the Lord has anointed me to bring good news to the afflicted; He has sent me

*Strong's Concordance #7121.

to bind up the brokenhearted, to *proclaim* liberty to captives and freedom to prisoners; to *proclaim* the favorable year of the LORD.

Isaiah 61:1–2 (emphasis added)

In the New Testament, the Greek word used for "proclaim" is *kēryssō*, meaning to publish, proclaim openly something which has been done, to proclaim after the manner of a herald, to announce.*

We see the word used in Mark 1:45 after the leper was cleansed by Jesus. Jesus had sternly warned him (in verses 43 and 44) not to tell anyone but rather to show himself to the priest according to the law, in order to be officially declared clean: "But he went out and began to *proclaim* it freely and to spread the news around" (emphasis added).

To proclaim involves boldness; it also means "to shout forth." As a new believer, I would often go out on the streets with a team and we would preach with boldness on street corners. Most of the time we would not have a sound system but would simply boldly invite people to come and hear "good news." We proclaimed (heralded, announced, proclaimed openly, shouted forth) the Gospel and invited those who rallied to receive prayer for salvation and healing.

While confession is often personal and even sometimes private, proclamation is public and much bolder. In its delivery, a proclamation is stronger and more official than a confession, even though both may contain similar content.

"Decree" Defined

A decree is an official order issued by a legal governmental authority. It is different from either a confession or a proclamation

*Strong's Concordance #2784.

30

in that it is brought forth through governmental initiation. In other words, a decree carries much more authority than does a confession or proclamation.

In the Old Testament, one Hebrew word commonly used for decree is *kathab*, which is defined as "a written edict of royal enactment, of divine authority."* We see an example of this word being used in Esther 8:8 (emphasis added):

> Now you write to the Jews as you see fit, in the king's name, and seal it with the king's signet ring; for a *decree* which is written in the name of the king and sealed with the king's signet ring may not be revoked.

This makes a decree made in the name of Jesus our King even more powerful, because He is for all eternity the King of all kings (see Revelation 19:16). There is no authority greater than that of Christ Jesus. And when you speak His Word, it carries incomparable weight and power—it will not be revoked!

Jesus taught that His Word will carry authority for eternity: "Heaven and earth will pass away, but My words will by no means pass away" (Matthew 24:35 NKJV). In Matthew 28:18, we see Jesus disclosing to His disciples that all authority in heaven and on earth had been given to Him and that consequently He wanted them to go out into the nations to make disciples. Because all authority has been given to Christ, His words have the last word; they are potent governmental words that His disciples can decree with confidence.

You will notice that in Esther 8:8, the decree was written and then signed off by the king with his seal. Christ's blood that was shed on Calvary seals our covenant with God.

*Strong's Concordance #3791.

The Bible is a book of God's written decrees that we can, in turn, decree with authority. Decrees made in the name of Jesus are always based on the truth found in God's written Word and are spoken with the bold, official, governmental Kingdom authority that has been granted believers through Christ. We have God's written Word! And we have the example of Jesus, who, when He was in the wilderness being tempted by the devil, responded to every temptation with, "It is written . . ." (Matthew 4:4, 7, 10). He was decreeing the Word in order to settle the issues of temptation that were being brought before Him.

When I began pulpit ministry in my twenties, I wrote a decree based on the Word and put it in my Bible. I would often decree into the various opportunities I had to preach: "It is written, 'The Spirit of the Lord is upon me and He has anointed me to preach good news to the afflicted and to bind up the broken-hearted. He has anointed me to proclaim liberty to captives and freedom to prisoners and has called me to proclaim the year of the Lord's favor'" (based on Isaiah 61:1–3). After forty years of preaching under His anointing, I can testify that those decrees were fulfilled in every aspect over and over again.

When we were ministering in the city of Tijuana in 1987, it was our desire to have open doors into the city jail and the prison so that we could share the Gospel with the prisoners and bring them food and aid. When we approached the authorities, they firmly denied us entrance. I sensed that the Lord was encouraging us to press in, and during prayer, He highlighted Isaiah 45:1–3 to my heart:

> Thus says the LORD to Cyrus His anointed, whom I have taken by the right hand, to subdue nations before him and to loose the loins of kings; to open doors before him so that gates will not be

shut: "I will go before you and make the rough places smooth; I will shatter the doors of bronze and cut through their iron bars. I will give you the treasures of darkness and hidden wealth of secret places, so that you may know that it is I, the LORD, the God of Israel, who calls you by your name."

These verses made a powerful impact on me. I wrote out a decree based on that Scripture and gave a copy to everyone on our team to use during our prayer time. In agreement, we declared:

In Jesus' name, we decree that the Lord opens doors before us in the city jail and in the federal prison so that their gates will not be shut.

He goes before us and makes the rough places smooth, shattering all resistance.

He gives us the treasures of darkness (souls, healings, deliverances) and hidden wealth of secret places (favor, grace, anointing) so that we know it is the Lord our God who calls us by name to fulfill this assignment.

We prayed it every day for a week in our prayer time and then went back to the jail and prison. In faith we took blankets, food, toiletries and Bibles to give to the prisoners. They welcomed us in and did not even make us go through security—this was supernatural favor! We spent hours in that dark place, reaching out to those who were bound and oppressed. Jesus' hope and love filled the place. Many were saved, healed and delivered, and we were welcomed back over and over. We never faced resistance in the jail or prison after that. The decree went to work on our behalf.

Hebrews 11:3 states that the worlds were "framed by the word of God" (NKJV). With the Word, we can frame situations we face in life. That is what happened in this situation. The

Word was sent before us and prepared the way. It fulfilled what it was sent to do.

Another Hebrew word translated as decree in the Old Testament is *gazar*, which means "a decree, to cut off, to destroy, to exterminate."* We find this word used in Job 22:28: "You will also decree a thing, and it will be established for you; and light will shine on your ways."

In this chapter we find Job's friend Eliphaz condemning Job, who had been going through a severe crisis for months. Eliphaz was misapplying a principle of God's truth, basically telling Job, "If only you would get yourself right with God, you would then be able to decree a thing and your problems would be cut off, destroyed and exterminated. Light would then shine on your ways and you wouldn't be in this mess you're in." (Have you ever had friends like this when you are in trouble? I hope not!) He accused Job of not having his heart right before God, but Job's heart *was* right; later we find God rebuking Eliphaz for this judgment and inaccurate representation of His heart toward Job (Job 42:7). However, the statement about the decree remains correct: When you "decree a thing, it will be established. And light will shine on your ways!"

When you make a decree, you are "cutting off, destroying and exterminating." This is a powerful way to engage in spiritual warfare. Decree the Word of God and let it go to work for you to destroy your enemies and their strategies. You will then be established in victory, and light will shine on your ways.

Early in my Christian walk, I was still working in my nursing career and caring for a patient who had overdosed on heroin. The medical staff I worked with did not have much hope for her, as she was a repeat offender and had almost died numerous

*Strong's Concordance #1504.

times. I went into her room and had a visit with her one evening. She was alone and felt hopelessly addicted. She admitted to me that all she could think of was going out to get another hit of heroin. Compassion rose up in me and I decreed: "In Jesus' name you are free from addiction. You shall live and not die, and declare the glory of the Lord" (based on Psalm 118:17). I could feel the power of the decree and so could she. That word went to work to destroy the addiction that had bound her. I led her to the Lord that evening and she was filled with the Holy Spirit and spoke in tongues. She was miraculously delivered from her addiction and did not suffer much in the process of withdrawal. Passionately, she began to walk with God, and she never returned to her old life. The decree had cut off, destroyed and exterminated her addiction, and the light of God shone on her ways from that time forth!

A woman who was introduced to the power of decrees was deeply grieved over her son. He had grown up in a Christian home and was filled with the Holy Spirit, but in his early twenties he was introduced to the "party scene," where there was much drinking, drug use and sexual promiscuity. Very quickly his life spiraled down. She prayed and prayed. She bound and rebuked the enemy's assignment on his life in Jesus' name and did everything she knew to bring her son back into alignment with the Word, but to no avail. His lifestyle deteriorated, and it caused her pain and great stress over many years.

After being introduced to the concept of decrees, she decided that she was not going to worry anymore but would simply send the Word forth in faith through regular decrees over her son. She repented from all stress, fear and anxiety about her son and left it up to God's Word to accomplish the breakthrough. Her son came into freedom in one night when the fire of the Lord burned within his heart. The spirit of conviction was so strong on him that he fully surrendered. He began to walk with the Lord again, and the calling that had been prophesied over his life when he was a child was restored. Following that breakthrough, the warfare over her son was ended—cut off, destroyed and exterminated. And light shone on all his ways.

God's Word, the Basis of Decree

Later in the book I am going to help you decree into specific aspects of your life. Jesus' words carry final authority in every area. Regardless of how devastating the circumstances look, God's Word will produce shifts when it is decreed in faith. (A decree spoken without faith is powerless.) Decree by decree, you will be settling issues in every area of your life.

Jesus said, "It is the Spirit who gives life; the flesh profits nothing; the words that I have spoken to you are spirit and are life" (John 6:63). When you decree the Word that Jesus speaks, you are releasing life and power in the situation you are decreeing into. Hebrews 4:12 (AMP) describes the active power available in God's living Word: "For the word of God is living and active and full of power [making it operative, energizing, and effective]. It is sharper than any two-edged sword."

His Word is:

1. living
2. active
3. full of power
4. operative
5. energizing

6. effective

7. sharp

Decree: Sending Forth the Word

When you decree the Word, it goes forth carrying out the purpose for which it was sent.

Let's take a look at the following Scripture verses and glean some valuable insights regarding decrees.

> For as the rain and the snow come down from heaven, and do not return there without watering the earth and making it bear and sprout, and furnishing seed to the sower and bread to the eater; so will My word be which goes forth from My mouth; it will not return to Me empty, without accomplishing what I desire, and without succeeding in the matter for which I sent it.
>
> For you will go out with joy and be led forth with peace; the mountains and the hills will break forth into shouts of joy before you, and all the trees of the field will clap their hands.
>
> Instead of the thorn bush the cypress will come up, and instead of the nettle the myrtle will come up, and it will be a memorial to the LORD, for an everlasting sign which will not be cut off.
>
> Isaiah 55:10–13

1. When the Word of God is sent forth, it accomplishes its mission—it will not return empty.

2. When the Word of God is sent forth, it releases breakthrough and accompanying joy.

3. When the Word of God is sent forth, it produces good fruit, the plantings of the Lord rather than thorns and thistles.

4. The breakthrough that the Word produces becomes a memorial to the Lord that will not be cut off.

I remember watching the Gulf War on television. It was the first televised war in history and, right before your eyes, you could see missiles being sent successfully to destroy their targets. A computer directed the path of the missiles to the actual target only. It was amazing to observe how the targets were hit with such precision.

Imagine the Word being sent through decrees to target an area of your life that is in need of breakthrough and release. That is what happens when you decree something; you send the Word to hit the target and it does just that: "So will My word be which goes forth from My mouth; it will not return to Me empty, without accomplishing what I desire, and without succeeding in the matter for which I sent it" (Isaiah 55:11).

The Creative Power of the Spoken Word

In the very beginning chapter of the Bible we see God's "Word power" at work:

> In the beginning God created the heavens and the earth. The earth was without form, and void; and darkness was on the face of the deep. And the Spirit of God was hovering over the face of the waters. Then God said, "Let there be light"; and there was light.
>
> Genesis 1:1–3 NKJV

The earth was in a state of chaos, emptiness and disorder. Darkness prevailed—but we also see the Spirit hovering over it. The Spirit and the Word worked together. The Spirit by Himself did not create the change; the spoken word did. The Spirit had been hovering over the darkness, yet there was still no light. However, as soon as the spoken word was released, light was created. I have heard some Bible scholars teach that the words "Let there be light" are more accurately translated *"Light, be!"* That is a decree, for sure!

With His spoken word, God proceeded to create the entire earth and universe.

Jesus, the Word . . . in the Beginning

This life-giving, creative Word that brought light into darkness in the beginning was Jesus Himself.

> In the beginning [before all time] was the Word (Christ), and the Word was with God, and the Word was God Himself. He was [continually existing] in the beginning [co-eternally] with God. All things were made and came into existence through Him; and without Him not even one thing was made that has come into being. In Him was life [and the power to bestow life], and the life was the Light of men. The Light shines on in the darkness, and the darkness did not understand it or overpower it or appropriate it or absorb it.
>
> John 1:1–5 AMP

Jesus, the Word, was released through God's voice into creation. His Light is in His Word, and as you proclaim His Word, you are releasing Jesus to create. When you decree, you are not just communicating some concepts or action points through the words you speak; you are decreeing the infusion of Christ's very life into the situations you are targeting. No wonder decrees are so powerful! "All things came into being through Him," and to this day, He is still the catalyst for all that continues to be called forth. He *is* the Word. When you proclaim His Word, His purposes take place. Light invades darkness. Atmospheres shift. He is the Eternal Word with all authority. He is the life-giving Word who creates and brings light into darkness and calls those things into being that did not exist (see Romans 4:17).

Calling Things into Being

Abraham did not have any children when God called him. Even though he and Sarah were in their older years, yet God spoke over Abram:

> Neither shall thy name any more be called Abram, but thy name shall be Abraham; for a father of many nations have I made thee. And I will make thee exceeding fruitful, and I will make nations of thee, and kings shall come out of thee.
>
> Genesis 17:5–6 KJV

The name Abraham means "father of a multitude" or "chief of multitude."* God decreed over Abraham that he was a father of a multitude when he had not produced even one child yet. He was decreeing it into being in the same way He called light into being in Genesis. In addition, every time Abraham spoke his own name, he was making a decree. He was calling himself a father of a multitude. Every time someone else called his name, they were also decreeing that he was a father of a multitude. Speaking of Abraham, Paul wrote: ". . . (as it is written, 'a father of many nations have I made you') in the presence of Him whom he believed, even God, who gives life to the dead and calls into being that which does not exist" (Romans 4:17).

When you decree, you call things that are not as though they are.

Annette Capps tells about her father, Charles, who called her to the kitchen one day where the table was piled with notes and mortgages—debts owed to the bank. He pointed his finger at the papers and said, "Notes, listen to me, I'm talking to you. In the name of the Lord Jesus Christ, I say to you, *Be paid in full*

*Strong's Concordance #85.

. . . Dematerialize . . . Depart . . . Begone . . . In Jesus' name, you will obey me!" Then, he just walked off.

Next, he drove to the property that was security for the debts and rolled down the window, shouting, "Listen to me! I am talking to you! Someone is impressed with you, and you will be a blessing to someone. I call you *'Sold'* in Jesus' name!"

He then drove off. He called things that were not as though they were, calling the property sold and the debts paid. Over the coming days, the property sold and all those notes and debts on the kitchen table were paid in full. Sure enough, debt was gone!*

He had decreed over them, calling those things that are not as though they are.

"Calling things that are not as though they are" is God's way of creating in our natural realm what He has already promised in His Word. This work of God's creative power can potentially replace and overthrow things in that natural realm that are unwanted.

Using the above example, we see that the decree nullified the debt and the bills by replacing them with provision and breakthrough. In the example of God decreeing "Light be" in Genesis 1:3, we see that the decree nullified the darkness and chaos by creating light.

Jesus often used this principle in His ministry. For example, we read in Luke 5:13 about a leper who had come to Jesus. He was full of devastating leprosy, but Jesus decreed, "Be cleansed." Immediately the leper was cleansed; his leprosy was gone. The decree of Jesus' word brought forth cleansing, healing and restoration that had not existed previously.

*Charles and Annette Capps, *God's Creative Power for Finances* (Tulsa, Okla.: Harrison House, 2004), 28–29.

Do *not* call things as though they "were not." For example, if you are fighting a sickness in your body, you should not decree, "I'm not sick; I'm not sick; I'm not sick!" In fact, you are sick. But that "fact" is subject to change. There is a difference between fact and truth. Facts are temporal (in the realm of time) and subject to change, while truth is eternal. It is important to acknowledge facts as facts, but it is more important to believe in and decree the truth. It may be a fact that you are sick, but it would be more advantageous to say that you are fighting sickness. You do not want to take ownership of being sick by declaring that you are sick, because such a declaration aligns with the devil's purposes; you could actually attract more sickness. Instead, you should powerfully decree the truth into this situation, "By the stripes of Jesus, I am healed!" With that, the healing power of God would go to work in your body and destroy the fact.

This separates the fact from the truth. You decree what is true according to God's Word while acknowledging the facts—which, remember, are only facts and therefore subject to change. You make a distinction between saying, "I am not sick" and "I am healed."

For example, if you had a large debt owed to the bank, you would not go to your banker and say, "I have no debt—I don't owe you anything." That would not be correct. In fact, that would be a lie, and you could cause yourself some big legal problems. Instead, you could speak the truth into the debt, decreeing, "God meets all my needs according to His riches in glory—I call this debt paid." By doing this, you are calling those things that are not as though they are. In the spiritual dimension, you are creating light in the midst of darkness. You are activating the Word of God and sending it forth to target the challenge. When the Word manifests, the fact will change—the debt will dissolve.

The principle of calling those things that are not as though they are is very exciting! If you "call it," the Word will go to work. Think about the potential for your life in the following scenarios.

Current Fact	Promise Decreed into Being
Sick	Healed
Depressed	Joy-Filled
Conflicted	At Peace
Rejected	Accepted and Favored
Poor	Rich
Lack	Plenty
Weak	Strong
Empty	Full
Cursed	Blessed

God's Word Is Incorruptible Seed

God's Word is referred to as incorruptible seed in 1 Peter: "For you have been born again not of seed which is perishable but imperishable, that is, through the living and enduring word of God" (1 Peter 1:23).

The rebirth took place in your life because when you heard the Word of God, you believed, and that Word entered your spirit and you became a brand-new creation. One moment you were a sinner, and in the next moment you became the righteousness of God through the entrance of His Word. God's Word made you a brand-new creation—old things passed away and all things became new in your spirit (2 Corinthians 5:17). The Word of truth you received created new life that did not exist before.

Negative Decrees

As previously highlighted in Esther 8:8, a decree carries governmental authority through the name of the king who issued it, and it shall not be revoked. A king is a ruler of a kingdom. Jesus is the ruler of His Kingdom, but Satan is also a king. He is the ruler of the kingdom of darkness. He understands the ways of the Kingdom of God and attempts to counterfeit them, and he is aware that the Kingdom is voice-activated. He is fully acquainted with the power of words because he is the "father of lies." If "king Satan" can successfully tempt you to speak a lie, then he is using you to decree a thing that will ultimately create evil and advance his kingdom.

Curses are released through the words that we speak. We must guard our words, because our words release either blessing or curse. Many people believe it does not matter what comes out of their mouths. Some will even say, "God knows I don't mean it." It *does* matter. Do not be deceived—every word matters!

A number of years ago, I was visiting someone from our local church. She was a lovely lady, but throughout our conversation she repeatedly said how "sick and tired" she was of various ongoing circumstances in her life. I knew she was referring to areas of agitation in her life and she did not mean to say that she was physically sick and tired, but it caught my attention because I had been learning about the power of words. At the end of our time together, I felt led to ask her if there was anything I could pray for before I left. She said, "Yes, please pray for my health. I've felt so tired recently, and I haven't been able to fully recover from the flu."

Oh my! I gently explained to her that she was constantly saying that she was "sick and tired," and that even though I understood she did not mean it literally, her words were cursing her. It was an uncomfortable moment for her when she realized it. I asked her to repent from the negative curse she was speaking over herself and to ask God to forgive her. We then prayed for the tiredness to go and for the flu symptoms to clear—and they did!

Long-Reaching Effects

You can see in this passage of Scripture that the words you speak not only affect you, but the blessing or curse they produce will also visit generations that follow: "I have set before you life and death, the blessing and the curse. So choose life that you may live, you and your descendants" (Deuteronomy 30:19).

Choose life. Decree God's Word.

When you worry or are fearful, you can easily end up speaking the devil's words. Out of the abundance of your heart, your mouth speaks. That's why Jesus constantly warned His people to "fear not" and to not be anxious. He knew that if worry and fear were in your heart, you would call forth what you fear. "From the same mouth come both blessing and cursing. My brethren, these things ought not to be this way" (James 3:10).

Let's heed the word that Paul wrote to the church at Ephesus: "Let no unwholesome word proceed from your mouth, but only such a word as is good for edification according to the need of the moment, so that it will give grace to those who hear" (Ephesians 4:29).

You are anointed of God to make decrees in the name of King Jesus that will create your world and advance His Kingdom. Your entire life can be transformed through the power of the decree that is in your mouth right now! "But what does it say? 'The word is near you, in your mouth and in your heart'— that is, the word of faith which we are preaching" (Romans 10:8).

Testimonies from Those Who Decree the Word

Financial breakthrough in my business

I knew if I paid my tithe this month I would not be able to make our entire payroll. So I went to the Lord in prayer and decreed, "Lord, your Word said to test You in this, so I'd like to do just that. You said if we bring our entire tithe into Your house that You would open up the floodgates of heaven and pour out so much blessing it could not be contained." So I decreed the scriptural blessing He promised and paid the entire tithe. The next day my employee told me they sold a product that was the exact equal to what I'd just tithed. Our sales jumped 32 percent by month's end. Needless to say I've learned the importance of and have enormous gratitude for always giving the Lord my first and best.

—Shirley Seger

God's miracle power released through decrees

One of my good friends was diagnosed with a rare cancer in her sinuses that is most commonly found in Asian men. She was told by her doctors that not only was this a rare, hard-to-identify cancer, but it was also very aggressive and that the prognosis of people who contract this cancer is very bleak. Most are only given two to five months to live. The name of the cancer is extra-nodal NK/T-cell lymphoma, nasal type. The "NK" stands for "natural killer."

While many were rallied to pray, my friend was still feeling the effect of this horrible cancer invasion in her body. She had major swelling, loss of teeth and a huge hole in her upper (maxillary) palate, preventing her from eating food. The doctors inserted a feeding tube because her ability to chew and swallow food was compromised as this hole grew bigger each day.

I felt led to call her and pray for her with decrees. When she answered the phone, she was receiving a chemo treatment. God told me to decree over her that the blood of Jesus flows through her veins and the same power that raised Jesus from the dead was swallowing up her cancer. I commanded the cancer to be swallowed up by Jesus' power and that it had to die immediately. My friend told me she was on fire, especially on her face and down her neck. She felt the healing taking place in her body. As I was decreeing over her, I was experiencing the power of the words and God's authority surging out of me, literally arresting this cancer.

About two days later, she went in the hospital for a scan to see if the cancer had spread to any of her organs or anywhere else in her body. The doctor came into the room with a shocked look on his face. His exact words were "your cancer is inactive." From the moment that my friend and I agreed and decreed, the cancer was arrested and her healing started. The medical consultants and doctors were soon retracing their earlier reports to see if she had been misdiagnosed.

My friend had an unusual cancer, but God did an unusual miracle and every part of her face, mouth and sinus cavity began to heal up. The power of decree released the healing into her body, and she will *live and not die, and declare the glory of the Lord.*

—*Cindy McGill*

Awarded government contracts

My husband and I wholeheartedly believe in making decrees! Our farm contract was up, with no other contracted work in sight. We prayed and decreed favor according to the Word of God. As we did this, not only did the atmosphere shift but our faith and authority went to another level!

The government called us and we were awarded not one but two five-year contracts with more opportunities to come! Making decrees is the way to go for breakthrough!! We continue to decree every day!

—*Roger and Susan Cheatham*

Supernaturally set free from a fifteen-year addiction to cocaine

I was in and out of jail, arrested over fifty times and on the streets doing the most demeaning things to get money for drugs. Thank God I had a praying mom! After praying for thirteen years, she started to decree the Word of God over me every day, until we finally got break-through! When I got clean in September of 2008, I began to decree these prayers over my own life, and deliverance started to take place!

My mind became renewed by the Word of God and I began to release my own testimony even as it was still taking place. I then started to decree over my three daughters that I had lost due to my addiction, and in the following years God worked miracles of restoration in my relationships with them. They are now all young adults and have beautifully blessed lives that I get to be a part of.

—*Ginger Brown*

From feeling powerless and fearful to feeling powerful and victorious

For many years, I was in a cycle of destruction with my daughter, Ginger, who was battling a fifteen-year drug (cocaine) addiction. For thirteen years into her addiction, I prayed, cried, grieved and brought her home many times only to have her run off again. When she would go to jail, she would turn to God for comfort, then relapse again and again upon being released. After so many times of trying and failing, we felt trapped by the enemy in a cycle of hopelessness that was completely overwhelming at times. It was a roller coaster of emotions.

At this point after praying relentlessly for thirteen long years, I quit praying for a short time, and the Lord then gave me a dream in which He spoke: "Pray and decree My Word until you see the salvation of the Lord."

So when I woke up, I was filled with new determination, but I asked God, "What am I doing wrong?" And I heard Him say, "You waver, and you are in the cycle of destruction with her. Step out of the cycle and keep your eyes on Me. Do not look at her and her present circumstances. Just decree My Word and believe My Word no matter what you see in the natural!"

So I began a two-year journey of faithfully decreeing His Word. At first things seemed to get even worse. The enemy kept trying to discourage me and tell me to give up, but I stood firm on what the

Lord had told me to do. Then, after two years I finally began to see her getting hungry for God and wanting to change her life.

God intervened, and Ginger became completely free from her addiction and lifestyle. Many miracles happened, including felony charges that were completely dismissed by the grace of God. Today she is whole, restored and blessed in the Lord. He has granted her the desires of her heart—mine too. The blessings just keep coming! Never give up! God's Word will never return void. It always accomplishes what it was sent to do.

—*Beverly Froman*

Decrees set the captive free

I received a call from a close relative who was heartbroken over his daughter's arrest and conviction on drug charges. She was looking at a forty-year sentence. In praying with him, I released the decrees, "I proclaim freedom for the captives and release from darkness for the prisoners; the Lord has brought you out of darkness and the shadow of death. He has broken your shackles" (Isaiah 61:1; Psalm 107:14). I continued to stand in these decrees with faith . . . and we saw a miracle! She was released from prison into a rehabilitation program. Today she is free in body and soul and is in ministry!

—*Michelle Burkett*

Mountain of debt removed

During a season of overcoming one mysterious health challenge after another, I felt led by God to seek treatment at a specialty clinic overseas. When I came back from the four weeks of tests and treatments, I had over $38,000 in medical debt spread out over several credit cards. I stood on the promise that God led the way, so He would also pay. Every day for a week I decreed that He would meet all my needs according to His riches in glory, and that He had dealt with my debt of sin at the cross, so He could also easily deal with my medical debts. The entire balance of $38,000 was miraculously paid for within the month. I didn't pay one cent of interest on the credit cards.

—*Robert Hotchkin*

Ministry acceleration through decrees

As I was pioneering a new ministry, I needed some breakthroughs. I wrote out decrees for all the breakthroughs I needed and promises that I felt God gave me for this new ministry. Each day in my prayer time, I would decree those decrees. Immediately, I started to see the decrees come to pass and my ministry accelerated.

—Elizabeth Tiam-Fook

Family member's salvation

When I received a call from my brother to come quickly to be at my dying father's bedside, I brought some written decrees with me and declared the promises of God daily for him. My father had aggressively opposed the Gospel his entire life, but God did a miracle and I was able to lead him to the Lord two days before he died.

—Ruth Brown

QUESTIONS TO PONDER

1. In Job 22:28, the original Hebrew word *gazar* means that with your decree, you are "cutting off, destroying and exterminating" so that light can come in. Is there a situation in your life (or perhaps of a loved one) where the enemy's intervention needs to be cut off, destroyed and exterminated? What is it? What would be a Scripture you can use in a decree to address this situation?

2. Review the lists in the table earlier in this chapter ("Current Fact" and "Promise Decreed into Being"). Are there any current troublesome facts in your life or a loved one's life? If so, what is a biblical promise that addresses that fact, which you can decree into being? (If there are several, choose one to write on the lines below.)

3. Do you recognize that you have been cursing yourself, a loved one or a situation inadvertently with your words? If so, repent. Write below how you will exchange those words of curse for words of blessing.

three

How to Prepare a Decree

You have the power of God's Spirit within you to transform your life and the world you live in. Decreeing God's Spirit-inspired Word enables you to call forth His purposes and to release His strength to destroy the enemy's works. God will always honor His Word, but He needs it released on the earth through His people.

Amos 3:7 reveals, "The Lord GOD does nothing unless He reveals His secret counsel to His servants the prophets." A prophecy is very similar to a decree, in that you are speaking forth God's inspired Word with faith and authority. In the Old Testament, prophets received God's Word and spoke it to the earth. When the Word was spoken, God moved upon it and fulfilled it. In the New Testament, all believers can receive the Word of the Lord (not only the prophets) and all believers can give His Word voice across the earth.

We are in partnership with God and commissioned by Him to bring His heavenly purposes into the earth. This was confirmed when Jesus taught His followers to pray in this manner: "Our Father who is in heaven, hallowed be Your name. Your kingdom come. Your will be done, on earth as it is in heaven" (Matthew 6:9–10).

Reading Genesis 1:27–28, we discover that God created humankind and gave them authority on earth. Due to humankind's fall into sin, we lost our place of executing earthly dominion, but Christ restored that severed authority to those who receive Him as Savior and Lord. He gave us permission to speak and act "in His name" (see John 14:13, 14; Mark 16:17; Matthew 28:18–20; John 20:21). In other words, we now have gained Christ's power of attorney—we represent Jesus Christ throughout the earth.

In Matthew 16:19 Jesus explained that He was giving power to those who believe in Him to act on His behalf on the earth. "I will give you the keys of the kingdom of heaven; and whatever you bind on earth shall have been bound in heaven, and whatever you loose on earth shall have been loosed in heaven."

Jesus promised that heaven would back His people up in whatever they bound or loosed on earth based on what He established through the New Covenant. In other words, if something was accomplished through His finished work on the cross, we His people have power to settle it on earth, while heaven backs us up.

We are positioned to win in our partnership with God! The Lord desires us to be successful in decreeing the Word, as we watch every decree bring forth the intended results. However, sometimes believers who step out to decree the Word get discouraged if the results do not seem to come as quickly as they had hoped. Why do we sometimes not see the immediate fulfillment of a decree? The following are some considerations that I will address in detail in the remainder of the chapter in order to help you to skillfully receive and deliver God-given decrees.

1. *Faith.* Lack of faith in God's Word, promise or ability can thwart fulfillment.
2. *Receiving the Word.* Failure to receive the accurate Word and the Father's perspective for the given situation can hinder the effectiveness of the decree.
3. *Delivering the decree.* Failure to deliver the decree can nullify the potential results from the decree.
4. *Power of endurance.* Lack of patience and endurance can result in a miscarriage of faith.

Faith

If you are going to be effective in making decrees, then you must absolutely believe the following as your foundation:

1. That God is all-powerful. All things are possible in Him (see Mark 9:23).
2. That God's Word ushers forth His will (see Genesis 1:3).
3. That God's Word has power to destroy the devil's plans (see Luke 10:19 and Jeremiah 23:29).
4. That God's Word is true and will come to pass when it is sent forth as a decree (see Job 22:28).
5. That you, as a believer in Christ, have the power and authority to decree His Word (see Matthew 28:18–20; Isaiah 59:21; Jeremiah 1:9).

God's Word is always true whether people believe it or not, but without faith, the Word will not be activated. As seen in Ephesians 1:3 and 2 Peter 1:2–3, every blessing and promise in the Word belongs to every believer, but many do not see these promises manifest in their lives because they fail to access the promises by faith.

I have heard people say, "I decreed God's Word but nothing happened—I do not believe that decrees work!" To confess such a conclusion is to say that you do not believe that God's Word is effective when decreed, yet the Bible teaches us that "God is not a man, that He should lie, nor a son of man, that He should repent; has He said, and will He not do it? Or has He spoken, and will He not make it good?" (Numbers 23:19).

We must never doubt God's Word. His Word carries final authority! Remember the simple application I shared in chapter 1: God said it. I believe it. That settles it!

Faith needs to be in operation in order for the Word to manifest. Let's use the following example to explain this. Jesus Himself said, "For God so loved the world, that He gave His only begotten Son, that whoever believes in Him shall not perish, but have eternal life" (John 3:16). This Word is absolutely true. No one needs to lack the gift of everlasting life, because it was given to everyone through Christ's finished work on the cross two thousand years ago. In this sense you could accurately say that on the cross, Jesus saved all mankind. He forgave. He became our substitute. He paid the full price. However, if there is no faith activated in an individual to connect to the amazing blessing of salvation, that person will actually perish. The criteria for fulfillment is that you *believe*. This goes for any promise in the Word.

Another example is found in Mark 11:24 where Jesus taught, "Therefore I say to you, all things for which you pray and ask, believe that you have received them, and they will be granted you." As Jesus explained in this passage, if *when* you pray, you believe that you have received—you have already received. He did not instruct His disciples to wait to believe until the answer to a prayer request was made manifest.

The nature of faith is that you already possess something before you see it. If you can already see it, then you do not need faith.

And the world was not made by things you can see—it was created by words. You cannot see the spoken word and you cannot see faith. You believe even when you do not yet see.

In John 20, we find Thomas refusing to believe that Jesus was resurrected unless he could feel the scars in His hands and the wound in His side. Jesus showed up in the midst of them and, in His mercy, invited Thomas to feel the natural reality. After Thomas felt them, he believed. Jesus then addressed him, "Because you have seen Me, have you believed? Blessed are they who did not see, and yet believed" (John 20:29). Faith is the internal evidence of what you cannot see in the natural.

Faith Is Not Hope

Faith is different from hope. Hope is futuristic, but faith is in the "now realm." Hebrews 11:1 teaches that "faith is the substance of things hoped for, the evidence of things not seen" (NKJV).

Hope is wonderful; it is a positive, joyful expectation that wells up within. But hope does not secure the promises of God—faith does. Hope is a springboard to faith, but faith is the very substance of what you hope for. It is the reality or evidence of what you cannot see in the natural yet.

When you are in faith, you already possess the promise. When you are in faith, it is settled within—you already possess it. Thomas was not in faith; we do not see that he had the internal reality of faith prior to touching Jesus' body. If your belief is based on what you have natural evidence for, then it is not faith.

Faith: Heaven's Currency

The day after I was born again, I shared my salvation experience with my New Age friends and I offered them the opportunity to receive Christ and have their sins forgiven too. They were politely enraged with my conversion and challenged me to the core. They wanted me to renounce my faith and they offered me some opposing beliefs to reason through. The problem was—it was too late. Faith had entered my heart already. They asked me how I could be so sure that Jesus made me a new person through the miracle of rebirth. It was an internal reality—I knew it! I did not need any outward signs; it was real and alive within. I had not read a Bible yet, nor had I undertaken any training, but I knew that I knew that I knew that Jesus was my Savior and that He had forgiven all my sins. I believed with all my heart that I was a new person within. Jesus' Spirit was dwelling within me. It made no sense to their natural minds, but that is the nature of faith.

That was in 1976 and nothing has changed since then. Faith connected me to this glorious promise of life in Christ, and His truth has been alive in me ever since. That is what faith does. Faith connects you to the truth and enables you to experience it.

Faith is heaven's currency. Without faith, we cannot please God, for we must first believe that He exists and that He rewards those who seek Him (see Hebrews 11:6). The righteous live by faith (see Hebrews 10:38). In Christ, all the promises have already been granted to everyone. That is why decreeing God's Word is so powerful. We are decreeing into the earthly realm the Word/promise that we already possess by faith so that it can manifest in the situation for which we send it.

As believers we should declare war on doubt and unbelief. They are deadly, and we tolerate them far too often. In James 1:6–8, we are warned that if we doubt God's will when we pray, we will be tossed about like the waves of the sea and will not receive anything from the Lord, being double-minded and unstable in all our ways. That is serious!

Once we know God's will, we must believe and not doubt. Israel had the sure word of the Lord when He promised them their own land that would flow with milk, honey and great abundance. Yet for forty years, they regularly doubted His word. Even when the twelve spies were sent in to scout out the land that was promised, they returned with a bad report. They were looking at the natural situation, not at the integrity of God's promise. Essentially, they were saying, "God, we know You promised us a good land, but we don't believe You—after all, look at the giants." When they looked at their circumstances, they never considered God or His promise to them. All they could see were giants, giants, giants. However, Joshua and Caleb came back with a different, faith-filled decree: "Let us go up at once and take possession, for we are well able to overcome it" (Numbers 13:30 NKJV).

The doubt and unbelief of God's people in the wilderness was addressed in the New Testament.

> "Today, if you will hear His voice, Do not harden your hearts as in the rebellion." For who, having heard, rebelled? Indeed, was it not all who came out of Egypt, led by Moses? Now with whom was He angry forty years? Was it not with those who sinned, whose corpses fell in the wilderness? And to whom did He swear that they would not enter His rest, but to those who did not obey? So we see that they could not enter in because of unbelief.
>
> Hebrews 3:15–19 NKJV

Let us not be unbelieving, but believing. When you see a promise in God's Word, choose to believe it—do not doubt it. Realize that if you decree a word that you do not believe, you are giving only lip service. Let faith fill you. Believe God and then decree the truth in fullness of faith.

Faith Is Based on Truth

I believe that the reason most people get trapped in unbelief is because they do not understand the difference between fact and truth. Here again is the difference: Facts are temporal (subject to the time realm) and truth is eternal. Facts are subject to change, but truth is not. Faith is based on truth and not on fact.

A medical diagnosis is always a fact and not the truth. A friend of mine was diagnosed with cancer. It was a fact that cancer cells had attacked her body, but the eternal truth was, by the stripes of Jesus, she was healed (based on 1 Peter 2:24). We prayed according to Mark 11:24 and received her healing by faith. Our decrees we made were based on the truth: By the stripes of Jesus she was healed. We were not waiting for her to be healed, as she was already healed according to how we prayed in obedience to Christ's instruction in Mark 11:24—we were simply waiting for the healing to manifest. We had already secured the promise in the spiritual realm and our faith was connected to the promise of God. We dealt with the facts as facts—her body had needs that we tended to—but we knew the difference between fact and truth. In the midst of caring for the facts (through various treatments, nourishment and practical care of her body), we stood on the truth with unwavering faith. After a number of months, she went back for testing and there was no trace of the cancer. She has now been cancer-free for years.

Another friend of mine was also diagnosed with cancer. Again, we were aware of the fact but stood on the truth with unwavering faith and love. We had received the healing by faith but were waiting for the manifestation of healing, which is a sure reality when you are standing in faith based on eternal truth. We knew that whether the manifestation came on this side of time or the other, it would manifest. We constantly decreed the Word over her and believed. While I have seen many healings manifest in the temporal realm while I stood on the eternal truth in faith, it did not happen this time; this friend passed into glory.

We did not see the manifestation of the truth on this side of time—but that does not make the truth any less true. When she passed over, her divine health manifested fully; there is no cancer in the eternal dimension. I do not understand why we do not always see the manifestation of promise on this side of time, but we know the truth is eternal and that only God's will and promises are manifested in the realm of eternity—there is no sickness, disease, poverty, lack, oppression or discord. We cannot shrink back from believing His Word and promises because of some disappointing experiences. One day we will fully understand. But for now, we need to stand in unwavering faith in the promises of God.

In Hebrews 11, we see that many of the heroes of faith went to their graves without seeing the manifestation of the promise of the Messiah. But their faith never wavered, and in the fullness of time, He was made manifest. From generation to generation they believed in the eternal truth, standing against everything that resisted their faith.

For decrees to be effective they need to be spoken with sincere faith and real conviction. Faith makes decrees work . . . decrees will not work without faith.

Receiving the Word

When you are facing a situation that needs to have God's will infused into it, or a battle that needs God's victory, go into His presence to receive the specific word of promise for that situation.

Jesus taught that if you ask, you will receive, if you seek, you will find and if you knock the door shall be opened to you (see Matthew 7:7). These are great promises: You will receive, find and have doors opened to you! This is what happens when you seek the Lord for His insight, wisdom and word for a particular situation.

While you are in His presence, He will reveal His perspective, His will and His promise to you. Too often we prefer to figure things out in our own minds. We lean to our own understanding rather than seeking the Lord. We could save ourselves a lot of trouble by going straight to the Lord.

Jesus said that He only spoke what He heard His Father speak (see John 12:50). He spent time in His Father's presence because He knew the importance of living His life from a heavenly perspective, even while He was living and ministering in the earth. One word from God can change everything in your life. No matter how impossible it might seem to you, whatever God speaks to you in His presence can be fulfilled! "For with God nothing is ever impossible and no word from God shall be without power or impossible of fulfillment" (Luke 1:37 AMPC).

Jesus taught that "man shall not live by bread alone but by every word that proceeds from the mouth of God" (Matthew 4:4 NKJV). The Scriptures are full of words born from the heart of God, but what word do you need for the specific situation you are facing? This word is received when you seek His presence. David, although an anointed king and a skillful warrior, often "inquired of the Lord" when he was in need of direction and breakthrough. Like David, you can inquire of the Lord and receive the specific word needed for your situation.

The following are some principles I use personally to seek the Lord. I am not suggesting that you follow them as steps into God's presence, as the Lord might direct you differently, but the principles I share might offer helpful encouragement to you.

When I Seek the Lord

When I seek the Lord, I follow these principles:

1. I believe that He is already present with me and that I do not need to strive to get Him to come to me.
2. I praise Him and engage in worship.
3. I pray using the gift of tongues.
4. I read the Word and meditate on it, inviting the Lord to speak to me through it.
5. I invite the Holy Spirit to lead and direct me, and I take note of what He speaks to my heart.
6. I apply what the Holy Spirit reveals to me and obey any instruction He gives.
7. I speak out the things the Lord reveals to me in the secret place.

First, *I believe that He is already present with me and that I do not need to strive to get Him to come to me.* My faith is all-important: "Without faith it is impossible to please Him, for he who comes to God must first believe that He is, and that He is a rewarder of those who diligently seek Him" (Hebrews 11:6 NKJV). Relationship with God is established through His grace and truth, not by works.

I do not strive for what I already possess. I do not follow by my natural senses but rather, I approach Him by faith. Sometimes I feel His presence as I seek Him, but most of the time, I do not feel Him—I simply believe He is there and that we are engaging in relationship together.

I do find it helpful to find a quiet time and place without distractions to focus on Him and His presence. This does not change things—He is already with me, and I am not waiting for Him to "show up." But it gives me the opportunity to attune my spiritual ears and enjoy this dedicated time with Him, as I would with a loved one, ready to listen.

Then *I praise Him and engage in worship*. This turns all my focus onto Him. I praise Him for the wonderful things He has done, and I worship and adore Him for who He is. This is what it means to worship Him in spirit and truth as Jesus taught (see John 4:24). As I worship Him, my entire being—spirit and soul—is engaged, while I proclaim truth about Him. This positions me to receive. I love adoring Him.

Praising and worshiping Him for what He has already done is also a great faith-builder. In the Psalms we see that David frequently recounted God's miraculous interventions in the past before calling upon Him for present situations.

Also, *I pray using the gift of tongues.** This has been a tremendous help to me. When you pray in tongues, your inner man is edified and strengthened. And I have discovered that I become more spiritually sensitive after praying in tongues (see 1 Corinthians 14:2, 4). During a session of seeking the Lord, I will often pray in tongues for a stretch of time—between fifteen minutes and two hours. Of course, even when my dedicated time

---

*Tongues is one of the nine gifts of the Holy Spirit outlined in 1 Corinthians 12:7–10. It is the supernatural ability to speak in a God-inspired language that you have never learned. All believers can speak in tongues.

of seeking the Lord needs to end, I can continue to seek Him and pray in tongues throughout the day and during my regular activities, even in a quiet whisper or under my breath if necessary. "Pray without ceasing," as Paul says (1 Thessalonians 5:17).

When I receive something from Him, I jot it down as soon as possible for later reference—even in the notes or voice app of my smartphone if that is all I have handy. I later review it, journal it and pray over it some more.

I take plenty of time to *read the Word and meditate on it, inviting the Lord to speak to me through it.* I study the Word and search the Scriptures for God's purpose, writing down specific promises that reveal His will (see Psalm 1:1–3 and 2 Timothy 2:15). There are many ways to approach the Word. For example, when you are seeking God for a breakthrough in an area, you can study His promises regarding that area of life. Today we have great Bible tools online that are easy to use, such as Bible concordances and dictionaries.

I was recently building a decree for personal revival. I simply went to the online concordance and typed in the word *revive* and read every Scripture in the Bible that included the word *revive*. I also looked up the words *revival, life* and *refresh* and studied those Scriptures. Through that experience of searching and studying the Scriptures, a few Scriptures excited me and gave me vision and faith for personal revival. Those are the ones I used to build my decree. This is often how the Holy Spirit will highlight words to you—you will feel an inner excitement or an "aha!"

I also like to read methodically through the Bible, one book at a time. I try to read a chapter or three per day. It is amazing how the Holy Spirit causes particular Scripture promises to "pop" as you read methodically. Often, promises are within the context of a story. As you read the circumstances of the Lord's promise (including, in many instances, its fulfillment), it will help build your faith. What He has done before He can—and will—do again.

Decrees must be built on the truth of God's Word and its promises to us. That is why we must search it out!

> It is the glory of God to conceal a matter, but the glory of kings is to search out a matter.
>
> Proverbs 25:2 NKJV

> The secret things belong to the LORD our God, but the things revealed belong to us and to our sons forever, that we may observe all the words of this law.
>
> Deuteronomy 29:29

Discovering promises is like being on a treasure hunt. At Christmas when our grandchildren were little, we hosted treasure hunts for them. The hunts began with giving them each a clue they followed. When they found the place that the first clue led them, there was another that led them to the next clue and the next. Finally, the last clue led them to the destination, the hiding place of their special gift. In this game, it was delightful to see them discover the final gift, but every stopping place along the way was great fun for them. Every clue they discovered was in itself a treasure. We did not hide the gift to keep them from finding it, but so that they would actually have the joy of discovering it through a fulfilling journey. In a similar way, God does not hide things from us; instead He hides things for us to discover. In His Word and His presence you will discover the treasures He has waiting for you!

When you receive a number of consistent promises in the Word for the desired area of breakthrough, expansion or establishment, you will understand God's perspective in that area.

The promises you have discovered are *yours* to stand on, to believe for and to receive. These promises are what you will build your decrees with.

Having sought the Lord up to this point, next *I invite the Holy Spirit to lead and direct me, and I take note of what He speaks to my heart* (see John 16:13). The Holy Spirit is present with us always, and He is our teacher and guide. He reveals truth to you and to me. He highlights things to our hearts.

One time while I was praying, the Holy Spirit brought to my mind a friend who, unbeknownst to me, was going through a struggle in her marriage. In my thoughts, I heard Him say, "Pray for your friend. Decree my victory over their marriage." I immediately made a decree of faith and victory, and then throughout the day it came back to mind a few times. I discovered later that there had been a serious issue. God had me intervene.

He wants to give us His divine perspective and intelligence. When we honor the Holy Spirit's role in our lives, He will lead and guide us into all truth and bring us into the fullness of God's plan for our lives.

Moving on, *I apply what the Holy Spirit reveals to me and obey any instruction He gives* (see 1 Samuel 15:22). I have found that the Lord will give more insight and instruction when I spend time with what He has shown me already. I try to be a good steward of it. I find that it helps to journal about insights and to act on what He speaks to me as soon as I am able.

In a devotion time early one morning, the Lord spoke to my heart, saying, "Go down to the park right now—I have a divine appointment for you." The park is a block from our home, so I grabbed a jacket and immediately obeyed. At the park, I looked for the "divine appointment." There was only one person in the park, so I assumed this must be the one: a woman probably in her late thirties sitting by the swings, looking a bit disheveled, smoking a cigarette. I approached her and initiated a conversation. She opened her heart concerning the desperate situation she was in. She was suicidal and without hope. Through our interactions that morning, she gave her heart to the Lord. I shared with her about how powerful God is and how, no matter what she was facing currently, God would walk her through into victory. I decreed breakthrough into her situation and brought her home with me. That encounter transformed her life. Her life turned around that day!

Responding to the Holy Spirit's instruction and promptings is important and can sometimes be a matter of life and death.

Last but not least, *I speak out the things the Lord reveals to me in the secret place* (see John 12:50). Receiving insights from God into your mind and heart is amazing, but when you speak them out, they are released in power into the atmosphere and into your life.

Sometimes, I simply will pray back to God what He gave me. For example, one of the Scriptures that was quickened to me when I was seeking Him regarding personal revival was Psalm 119:25: "[O Lord,] Revive me according to Your word" (NKJV). Immediately, I prayed that very word back to God using my *voice* to deliver the prayer. James teaches us that our words direct the course of our life (see James 3:3–5). That is why giving voice to the revelation God gives you is so powerful.

At other times I will immediately decree the Word into the situation I am believing for. Recently, I was praying for the financial needs of a ministry project we were working on. I had previously sown a financial gift into another ministry, believing God to bless them and to receive the return on "the seed" that would then meet our needs. While in prayer one morning, I was quickened to speak forth the following Scripture that the Holy Spirit highlighted: "In Jesus' name, I call forth thirty, sixty and a hundredfold increase on the seed I sowed." This was based on Mark 4:20, but I gave voice to it immediately in the form of a single decree. Our needs for the project were more than met. The Word went forth and produced a harvest.

You can speak forth the insights He grants you in His presence through prayer and verbal decrees. The more you speak each one, the more you will remember them. It is one thing to have an insight given into your mind, but what helps to powerfully establish it in your life is speaking it out loud. Later in this chapter, I will reinforce the importance of giving voice to your decrees.

Obtaining Heaven's Perspective

When you spend time in His presence, you will begin to understand heaven's perspective. When you consider adverse situations or seemingly impossible invitations from the Lord, it is easy to get overwhelmed and lose perspective. God always wants you to look at your situation through His eyes. He is big and powerful and nothing that you face in life is too much for Him to handle. In fact, it is easy for Him!

I remember a time years ago when I had just begun television ministry, and I was overwhelmed with the amount of financial provision I needed to believe God for every month. Our monthly ministry budget doubled overnight when we started television production, and it was a massive stretch for my faith at the time. Every month we barely met the needs. One night, I could not sleep, as I was distressed. Within a couple of days, I was going to need a large amount of money to pay the bills, and there was not a dollar in sight. I went out to the hot tub early in the morning while still dark and poured my complaint out before God. "O God, I need $80,000 within two days," I wailed. "But, O God, even if You meet *this* need, I will need more again *next* month." I continued to cry and whine . . . and then finally sank into silent despair. That is when God spoke. He assured me that He was big enough to meet all my needs and that even if it were millions, billions and trillions, it would still be nothing for Him. He reminded me of how He clothes all the flowers of the field and feeds all the birds in the whole wide world every single day and is never anxious for even a fraction of a second.

I realized that I was locked into a restricted, earthly mindset filled with fear and uncertainty in the face of my challenges, but that God was operating from a heavenly perspective. When you look at things from a heavenly, eternal perspective, everything looks different. All things are possible with God! The victory has already been secured through Christ.

I came out of the hot tub decreeing, "My God shall meet all my needs according to His riches in glory by Christ Jesus" (see Philippians 4:19). I met with my team later that morning and shared with them God's promise, which we decreed together. Sure enough, all the funds came in, just in time, and they continued to come in every month and every year following, even though the budget greatly increased over the years. I had received His Word and His perspective so that when I decreed, I was full of faith; faith had been birthed into my heart while in His presence. I learned that His promises work not only for a small amount of need, but also for a large amount. The Word is never overwhelmed with a circumstance.

You are seated in heavenly places in Christ (see Ephesians 2:6)—that is throne-room positioning! In Colossians 3:1–3 Paul teaches us to be mindful of our heavenly position in Christ:

> Therefore if you have been raised up with Christ, keep seeking the things above, where Christ is, seated at the right hand of God.

Set your mind on the things above, not on the things that are on earth. For you have died and your life is hidden with Christ in God.

Why embrace limited and failing earthly perspective when you can gaze from the throne-room perspective? His Word reveals His perspective.

Writing a Decree

When you are preparing a decree, identify the specific area that you want to target with God's Word. This is important because you will be sending the Word forth and you will want it to hit the mark. For example, if you need breakthrough in the area of provision, then study the promises of God regarding provision. Gather them together and write them out. Which ones do you feel excited about in your spirit? Which ones do you feel your faith connecting to? Those are the ones you will want to use.

Decrees do not have to be long to be powerful. In fact, sometimes shorter decrees, declared over and over, have more power than longer ones. Be led of the Spirit.

For my personal devotional purposes, I usually write decrees in first person, because I am making the decrees over my own life. As I am making the actual declaration, it is easy to change it to make the decree over others or over specific situations.

My prayer team leaders often write decrees that target the birthing of a specific mandate or breakthrough and distribute them through email to a large base of intercessors who come into agreement.

The intercession leader at our church writes decrees and posts them on the media screens for the congregation to declare together on Sunday mornings during pre-service prayer—it is very powerful as we read them out together in one accord.

We at times prepare written decrees for our ministry partners printed on flyers so they can use them to decree the blessings over their lives and families. When we do this together the results are amazing, as we are all agreeing on the same decrees.

We have also often written prophetic decrees and posted them on social media portals for many to declare en masse, sending the word into the earth to bring about shifts.

I know many who keep a file of specific decrees they have written. I have personally written and published many decrees in books that I use during my own prayer and devotion times, and they have also been used as a helpful tool by many. In the next section of this book you will find many useful decrees that will minister into various areas of your life.

Delivering a Decree

The Kingdom of God is voice-activated, so decrees need to be spoken. In the same way that God spoke the world into existence, we can be His voice today, for He is still creating. He needs your voice. All the promises in the Word are available to every believer, but none of them will be activated unless they are given voice, even as shared earlier in this book regarding the time of creation. We find the Spirit of God brooding over the darkness and chaos, but light was not formed until God's voice spoke His Word, "Let there be light."

Many words are lying dormant today because they are not voice-activated. You are God's voice in the earth. *You* are to send forth His Word to create His will in the natural realm.

God's Word is eternal, and He is looking for a voice in the earth to activate it. The voice of the Lord is powerful. When you give voice to God's truth, look at what can happen.

Here are some wonderful verses from Psalm 29 that confirm the power of God's voice.

> The voice of the LORD is powerful; the voice of the LORD is full of majesty. The voice of the LORD breaks the cedars, yes, the LORD splinters the cedars of Lebanon. . . . The voice of the LORD divides the flames of fire. The voice of the LORD shakes the wilderness; the LORD shakes the Wilderness of Kadesh. The voice of the LORD makes the deer give birth, and strips the forests bare; and in His temple everyone says, "Glory!"
>
> Psalm 29:4–5, 7–9 NKJV

We also discover in another psalm that giving voice to the Lord's Word activates angels: "Bless the LORD, you His angels, mighty in strength, who perform His word, obeying the voice of His word!" (Psalm 103:20).

Are you giving voice to God's authoritative Word? If you are not giving God's truth a voice, instead you might be giving the enemy's lies a voice. For example, if you declare, "I am so weak, so rejected, so tired . . . ," you have given voice to the enemy's desires. Oftentimes, after watching the evening news, people will confess how terrible the world is and begin to affirm the bad state of affairs. Doing that gives the enemy's intentions a voice. In order to penetrate the darkness with light, we need to intentionally decree into the darkness, not support it and give it our agreement.

The more we deliver decrees of God's Word, the more we will see the manifestation of His glory in the earth. Let's be His voice!

Using Decrees in Prayer

According to Revelation 1:6, you are a king and a priest for God in the earth. You are a king serving the King of kings. You are a priest serving the great eternal High Priest. Further confirmation is found in 1 Peter 2:9 where we are referred to as God's "royal priesthood." As a king and priest before God, you have authority to speak in His name, bringing heaven to earth through decrees of His truth.

In Numbers 6:22–27, we see the example of the Lord giving instruction to His priests to make decrees of His will over His people.

> Then the LORD spoke to Moses, saying, "Speak to Aaron and to his sons, saying, 'Thus you shall bless the sons of Israel. You shall say to them:
>
> 'The LORD bless you, and keep you; the LORD make His face shine on you, and be gracious to you; the LORD lift up His countenance on you, and give you peace.'
>
> "So they shall invoke My name on the sons of Israel, and I then will bless them."

You can see in these verses how this powerful decree made by the priests was intended to work: God had them decree the word of blessing over His people, and as a result, He would bless those they decreed over. If the Word was declared, God could act. The same results will come in our day when God's priesthood declares His blessing over His people.

When God's Word is conceived in your heart, then formed by the tongue and spoken out of your own mouth, it becomes a spiritual force releasing the ability of God within you.*

Ephesians 3:20 addresses "Him who is able to do far more abundantly beyond all that we ask or think, according to the power that works within us." God is able to do things beyond your wildest imagination, but His power in you needs to be unlocked. His ability to accomplish His will in the earth is

---

*Charles Capps, *The Tongue a Creative Force* (Tulsa, Okla.: Harrison House, 1976), 7.

"according to the power that works within [you]." The power that works within you is activated through giving Him voice.

When You Are Preparing a Decree

In times of prayer when you are seeking God for the fulfillment of needs or for breakthroughs, you will find decrees a powerful tool. The following is a practical guideline to preparing effective decrees in prayer and intercession.

1. Clearly define the issue to be settled or created.
2. Believe that God's Word is the final authority—not the circumstances or facts.
3. Search for God's Word and will regarding the circumstance.
4. Write it out.
5. Decree in unwavering faith and conviction that the Word decreed will not return void but will accomplish what it is sent to do (see Isaiah 55:11).

Decrees are powerful when there is only one person decreeing them, but when you share the decree with others in a prayer meeting, family devotional time or other gathering and have them decree it also, this increases its effectiveness. There is power in agreement: "Again I say to you, that if two of you agree on earth about anything that they may ask, it shall be done for them by My Father who is in heaven" (Matthew 18:19).

Singing a Decree

Many of the psalms were actually decrees of truth that were intended to be sung out congregationally. Singing decrees is powerful! My friend Julie Meyer teaches believers how to sing the Word. I have always loved decreeing the Word, but when I started to sing it, I broke through into new levels of faith and effectiveness. (I must admit, though, that I prefer to sing my decrees privately before the Lord, which makes it easier on others who may be listening!)

Julie discovered through her research that when you sing, you are actually engaging both the creative and logical parts of the brain at the same time, which means that when you sing words, they are easier to remember. For example, Alzheimer's patients might not remember names, people, times or events, but they will often remember songs and sing them from beginning to end perfectly.

Try singing your decrees and do not worry about whether you think your voice is pleasant or not—in God's presence, your voice is altogether lovely!

In the next section of the book, I am going to show you how decrees can transform specific areas of your life. Jesus taught in Mark 4 that the Word is like seed that we sow, and when it is sown, it can yield up to thirty, sixty and even a hundredfold return. Imagine your life, filled with the abundant fruit of the Word you decree. I think it might be time to start decreeing!

Forever, O Lord, Your word is settled in heaven.

Psalm 119:89

Testimonies from Those Who Decree the Word

New truck

Our family needed a truck, and so we began researching the kind of truck that we thought would serve our family well. We found what we liked, down to the last detail: a charcoal grey Dodge Ram 1500 with a quad cab. Each day, as a family, we would decree and declare a new truck.

One night, following an amazing revival meeting, someone drove up next to me in the parking lot. I couldn't see his face because of the light shining behind him. He asked me what kind of car I was believing God for. Without knowing him, I gave him the exact details of his own work truck, including the very color and year. The man invited my family and me to come to his house, where he and his family gave to us a gorgeous, recently detailed 4x4 charcoal grey Dodge Ram 1500 with a quad cab, along with a $100 bill to help cover an oil change. We've now had the truck for five years and haven't had any problems. It has been such a wonderful blessing to our family.

—*Darren Stott*

Conquering a challenge as newlyweds through decrees

When my wife and I first got married, we faced some financial challenges. For two years we decreed the Word of God over our finances. We got the breakthrough and now we continue to stand and decree that we have seed from God to sow and are blessed with abundance! Decree a thing and it will be established!

—*Russell Maynard*

Strength for each day

I have a health condition that I am addressing with faith-filled decrees. As I am waiting for the manifestation of my healing, I need strength each day in order to accomplish daily tasks, as severe physical weakness is one of the things I battle. I began decreeing, "As my days are so shall my strength be." Since decreeing daily, I have been able to accomplish daily tasks as well as attend exercise classes three to five times per week.

—*Ronald Cocking*

A blessed marriage

Everyone told us that the first year of marriage can be especially challenging when you come together in the second half of life since both people are so set in their ways. But my fiancée and I sought the Lord for Scriptures we could declare to frame and establish our marriage in the Spirit before we stepped into it in the natural. We came up with fourteen decrees and prayed them daily for several weeks before our marriage ceremony. Our first year of marriage was the opposite of challenging. It was glorious!

—Robert Hotchkin

God gave me a beautiful marriage and children

After decreeing for a good Christian husband for a few years, I met and married the most amazing man in December of 2012. He did not have any children, and due to my own previous long-term drug addiction and life of crime, my tubes had been tied after my third daughter was born in 1998.

Before we married, I was honest with him about this since he did not have children of his own. I told him there was a surgery we could have to put my tubes back together, but there was less than a fifty percent chance of this working. (I truly believed God had told me in the year that I got clean that He was going to give me another child.) He said we could do the surgery if I wanted to, but he still wanted to marry me either way.

I became pregnant about five months into our marriage while my tubes were still tied, and I thought this would be our miracle, but we lost that baby about six weeks in. Since that baby had probably been trapped outside of my womb, we went ahead and had surgery to fix my tubes a few months later. I then began to decree the Word of God over my womb and pray into the word I had heard from Him years before, firmly believing He would give us a child.

Over the next six months following my tubal reversal, we had several challenges, but I reminded myself of what the Lord told me and continued to pray, decree and believe for our miracle. Through a number of "divine interventions," I became pregnant with twins. They were born in February of 2016 . . . a boy and a girl! Our cup runneth over. My life has been blessed beyond anything I could have ever imagined. I thank God every day for all my many blessings and I continue to decree the Word of God over my life and family.

—Ginger Brown

A life turned around

My son-in-law was in a coma and three neurologists told my daughter he would probably not make it. We prayed for my son-in-law and declared life over him. We decreed that he would live and be whole. He came out of the coma as a good, loving person. For the first time in our relationship with him, we talked about God, and now he sees things so differently. He had previously been a self-proclaimed agnostic.

—*Deborah Quinn*

Decrees saved my hand from being scarred

One day, I accidently poured boiling water over my hand. I decreed the Word of God, declaring that there would be no burn effects or blisters on my skin. My hand was perfectly fine and did not even turn red!

—*Cindy Stewart*

Multiplication and increase in career advancement

I decreed multiplication and increase in financial and career advancement over my son-in-law. In a short time following, he was called by a company that wanted to hire him, and they offered much more money than he was making!

—*Rivka Napenda*

QUESTIONS TO PONDER

1. Faith is key to seeing results when we decree the Word. At the beginning of the chapter, five required areas of faith are mentioned. Do you struggle regarding your "faith level" in any of these areas? Write them down,

and next to each one write out the accompanying Scriptures that back it up. Sometimes it is helpful to write them in your own words (paraphrase) for deeper understanding. Meditate on the Scriptures and speak them out until they are ingrained within you.

2. Is there any situation in your life (or a loved one's life) for which you recognize that you need heaven's perspective? Spend some time in the Lord's presence and search out several Scriptures that would address this situation. Based on what you have learned in this chapter, write them as a decree.

3. What was God's instruction to Aaron and other priests regarding Numbers 6:22–27? What would be His response to their decreeing this blessing? If you, as a priest over your family, decree this blessing over them, what are some manifestations of God's response that you can expect?

BENEFITS OF DECREES

The powerful, eternal Word of God is well able to influence and transform your life. In Christ you have an eternal and unbreakable covenant, and as a result, all His promises are "Yes" and "Amen" (see 2 Corinthians 1:20).

Daily decrees of the Word will strengthen your inner man and prepare you for every good work. In the following section, you will enjoy specific decrees prepared for various areas of your life. Let's review the wonderful benefits of decrees.

The Word of God . . .

> . . . is eternal in the heavens and never changes (see Matthew 24:35).
>
> . . . will not return void but will accomplish its assignment (see Isaiah 55:11).
>
> . . . frames the will of God in your life and all that pertains to you (see Hebrews 11:3).
>
> . . . dispatches angels (see Psalm 103:20).
>
> . . . expels darkness (see Psalm 119:130).
>
> . . . is a lamp to your feet and a light to your path (see Psalm 119:105).
>
> . . . secures blessings in your life (see Ephesians 1:3; 2 Peter 1:3).
>
> . . . is seed that will produce a great harvest when sown (see Mark 4:3–23).
>
> . . . is our weapon of warfare (see Ephesians 6:10–20; 2 Corinthians 10:3–5).
>
> . . . pulls down evil and carnal mindsets (see 2 Corinthians 10:3–5).
>
> . . . creates (see Romans 4:17).

. . . sanctifies (sets you apart for God) (see John 17:17).

. . . strengthens your spirit man (see Ephesians 5:26).

. . . ensures answers to prayer (see John 15:7; 1 John 5:14–15).

In the next section of the book, I am going to show you how decrees can transform specific areas of your life. Jesus taught that the Word is like seed that we sow, and when it is sown, it can yield up to thirty, sixty and even a hundredfold return (see Mark 4:1–20). Imagine your life, filled with the abundant fruit of the Word you decree. "Forever, O LORD, Your word is settled in heaven" (Psalm 119:89).

Enjoy the spiritual strengthening you will receive through the following devotional teachings and Word decrees that target specific areas of your life. It is time to start decreeing!

PART TWO

DEVOTIONS
and
DECREES

Worship and Adoration

The Lord has commanded His people to love Him with all that is within them and to write those words on their hearts and to teach them to their children.

> "Hear, O Israel! The LORD is our God, the LORD is one! You shall love the LORD your God with all your heart and with all your soul and with all your might. These words, which I am commanding you today, shall be on your heart. You shall teach them diligently to your sons and shall talk of them when you sit in your house and when you walk by the way and when you lie down and when you rise up. You shall bind them as a sign on your hand and they shall be as frontals on your forehead. You shall write them on the doorposts of your house and on your gates."
>
> Deuteronomy 6:4–9

Even to this very day, Jewish families have this Scripture posted on the doorposts of their homes as a reminder to always keep God as their first love and first priority.

When your heart's first and primary affection is for God, then everything else comes into alignment. Jesus taught this also in the New Testament: The first and greatest commandment is "love the Lord your God with all your heart, and with all your soul, and with all your mind, and with all your strength" (Mark 12:30), and the second involves loving others. This is His divine order.

When you love God before all else, the following blessings will fill your life:

1. You become like Him—you become like the one you adore.

   When your heart is filled with affection for the Lord, you will take on His character, nature and attributes. When I was growing up, I remember that my mother taught me to choose my friends wisely. She would say, "You will become like the company you keep." People usually do not find themselves copying the behavior of those they do not like or those they despise, but they do take on the characteristics of those they admire and love.

   The more you get to know God, the more you love Him, and the more you love Him, the more you become like Him.

2. You are able to love yourself and others.

   First John 4:19 states that we love because He first loved us. When we purpose to love God above all else, He gives us the ability to love ourselves and ultimately to love those around us. God *is* love and we are made in His image. It is very difficult to love God with all your heart, mind and strength and not love others. In fact,

Scripture reveals that "the one who does not love does not know God, for God is love" (1 John 4:8). It further teaches: "If someone says, 'I love God,' and hates his brother, he is a liar" (1 John 4:20).

3. You naturally walk in ways that are pleasing to Him.

When you worship, your heart is turned toward Him and you become aligned to His ways and purposes. Following worship, you experience an ease in your spiritual walk. Often, when pondering the power of this alignment, I think of Daniel. In the book of Daniel, we discover that he and his friends were uncompromised worshipers, and we also see that they were uncompromised in their walk with the Lord. When you worship "in spirit and truth" (John 4:24), you will experience a precious consecration unto the Lord. In that "set-apartness" you discover grace that leads you in His paths.

4. You receive insights and revelation from His heart.

Often during times of worship I find that insight and revelation fill my heart concerning Kingdom truths and specific assignments I have been given. In the first chapter of Revelation, we find John exalting Jesus Christ. During his time of focus on the Lord, he went into realms of deep revelation, divine knowledge and understanding. A posture of worship positions you to receive supernatural wisdom and revelation.

Decrees of worship will help you worship. I often begin my devotion time with a decree of worship, as it helps me to focus. Life is full of distractions, and sometimes we just feel empty and dry and lacking motivation to worship. I have discovered that as I decree my adoration and exaltation of God, it opens my heart to a sweet connection with Him. As I declare worship decrees, I find that my heart is drawn into His, and more worship begins to flow spontaneously from my soul. Decrees of worship become a springboard to deep worship flowing from a passionate heart. It is a great way to begin the day!

QUESTIONS TO PONDER

1. Do you have a dedicated time every day to worship the Lord? If not every day, how often? What are ways in which you express your worship to Him?

2. In what ways has worship changed you personally—your character, the way you see yourself, the way you relate to others?

3. What are some insights and revelation that you have received directly from the Father during your times of worship?

_____

_____

_____

_____

Decree

Worship and Adoration

Heavenly Father, I devote myself to You this day in spirit, soul and body. I love You with all my heart, mind, soul and strength. My life is set apart for You and for Your purposes.

As I confess and decree Your Word, Your Holy Spirit helps me to be a passionate worshiper, a lover of truth and a faithful child who brings pleasure to Your righteous heart.

I worship You in spirit and in truth. Along with the host of heaven, I declare:

Holy, holy, holy, Lord God Almighty, who was and is and is to come!

You are worthy, O Lord, to receive glory and honor and power; for You created all things, and by Your will they exist.

Blessing and honor and glory and power be unto Him who sits on the throne, and to the Lamb, forever and ever!

Holy, holy, holy is the Lord of hosts; the earth is full of His glory!

You, O Lord, are sitting on Your throne, high and lifted up, and the train of Your robe fills the temple. I ascribe greatness to You, for You are my God and my Rock. Your work is perfect, and all Your ways are just. You are a God of faithfulness—righteous and upright and without injustice.

I love You, O Lord my God, with all my heart, mind and strength. You are the Lord, and there is no other. There is no God besides You. I glory in Your holy name, and my heart rejoices in You. I will seek Your face evermore! I bless You, O Lord, my God. You are very great. You are clothed with honor and majesty.

While I live, I will praise You. I will sing praises to You while I have my being. The high praises of God will be in my mouth and a two-edged sword in my hand.

> Praise the LORD! Praise the LORD from the heavens; praise Him in the heights! Praise Him, all His angels; praise Him, all His hosts! Praise Him, sun and moon; praise Him, all you stars of light! Praise Him, you heavens of heavens, and you waters above the heavens!

Scripture references used in this decree

Mark 12:30; John 4:24; Revelation 4:8–11; 5:13; Isaiah 6:1, 3; Deuteronomy 32:3–4; Mark 12:30; 1 Samuel 2:1–2; Psalm 105:4; 104:1, 33; 149:6; 148:1–4 [NKJV]

Love

Your Creator, God, is love. Therefore you were created by love, in love and for love. Knowing and experiencing God's love is the most important foundation stone for your growth in Christ and for your well-being in life. You were created to be loved and to love others—it is an essential need for all human beings. Everyone is looking for it, and many have taken great risks, engaging in harmful and even fatal compromises, in order to receive it.

The Word teaches you who you are and what you have in Christ, and it clearly reveals that you are eternally loved with God's unconditional love. His love for you is not based upon your performance but on His choice to love you with a perfect love no matter what.

The night I was born again in 1976, I was filled with the tangible presence of His love. It felt like a warm liquid filling my soul, and in an instant it removed all guilt, condemnation and shame from my life. Even though I had nothing worthy to offer

God that night and my behaviors at the time definitely did not warrant such a gift, He did not hesitate to lavish me with His rich, unconditional love . . . and He has never stopped! His love transformed me in that moment and His love continues to do so. He offers this to everyone He creates—He offers it to you. When you are loved, you see everything through a different lens—His lens.

The enemy works overtime to keep us from understanding and receiving God's love because he knows how powerful we are when we know God's love. He cruelly plagues humankind by setting each of us up to receive soul-damaging assaults of fear, condemnation, criticism, anger, rejection, betrayal, abandonment, slander, offense, unforgiveness and bitterness. All of this buffeting will separate us from the life-giving knowledge of His love if we do not know the truth about how perfectly we are loved by God.

One night as we were ministering in an inner city, I stopped to share God's love with a girl who was "working the streets" as a prostitute. I invited her to join me for a quick break in a coffeehouse we hosted. Our mission was to help the girls on the street receive freedom in Christ. The outreach post was situated in a small mall behind the main street, where the girl's pimps could not easily locate her. She was shaking with fear as I led her into our little place of refuge, but as our team shared God's love with her, the shaking subsided. Hope entered her heart and peace calmed her body.

She opened up to us with her story. Unfortunately, she was one of many through whom we had heard similar stories. She shared how her pimp would beat her with fiery-hot coat hangers if she did not bring in enough money. He had often whipped her back until it bled, and had placed her hands on burning stove elements or withheld food and drugs from her until she made her "quota" for the night.

Her story was a sad story of abuse and abandonment from childhood, and we realized that even from birth she had never experienced love . . . until that night! God's tangible presence of love filled the room, and He filled her. She was born again that evening. We made declarations of God's love over her, and more of His presence filled her. Even though this was many years ago, I can still remember her expression of joy. She testified, "This is better than any drug I've ever taken." And then she laughed and laughed and laughed.

That night we were able to hide her from her pimp and make arrangements to fly her out the next morning to a different location in the nation where we hosted a house for girls who were coming out of similar situations. In that place, love delivered and healed them as skilled workers guided them through their restoration process. She did well in the program and was not only set free from her hellish past, but she also grew in love and in life skills over time and was positioned for success and fruitfulness. Love made the difference!

One of the primary tools that will establish the love of God in your life is to decree His truth concerning His love. I have met many who struggled to believe they were loved by God, so they continued to live with condemnation, guilt, shame, rejection and fear. However, when they found the wonderful tool of decreeing God's love, their lives were transformed. Over time, the enemy's lies weakened until they lost their power to harm or restrict.

The more you decree the Word regarding God's love in you and through you, the more you will grow in experiencing God's love for you and in expressing your love to God. Then you will be able to bless others with His rich love that flows through you. The more you decree God's love, the more filled with it you will be!

QUESTIONS TO PONDER

1. Have you had encounters with God or other experiences that have helped you feel His love in a special, new way or have given greater personal revelation about His love for you? What was revealed to you about His love?

2. How has experiencing and leaning into God's love helped you love others?

3. What are a couple of Scriptures about God's love that especially speak to you, and why?

Love

The Lord loves me with an everlasting love and has promised to give me a future and a hope. With lovingkindness He has drawn me to Himself. I look carefully and intently at the manner of love the Father has poured out upon me. It is through this love that He has called me to be His dear child. I am completely and fully accepted in Him, my God and Savior.

Nothing can separate me from the love of God that is in Christ Jesus my Lord—not tribulation or distress; not persecution, famine or nakedness; not peril, sword, angels, principalities or powers; not death nor life; neither things present nor things to come—absolutely nothing can separate me from the love of God which is in Christ Jesus my Lord.

God's love toward me is patient and kind. His love for me bears all things, believes all things, hopes all things and endures all things. His love will never fail. His love for me is so rich that He gave His only begotten Son on my behalf.

Because of this, I will never perish but will have everlasting life with Him. As a result of God's great love for me, I have an unbreakable, eternal covenant with Him. Through this covenant of love, He has put His laws within my heart and has written His commandments upon my mind.

I have been invited to the Lord's banqueting table, and His banner over me is love. His love is better than the choicest of wines. Through His intimate love, He draws and invites me to follow after Him. I am fair and pleasant to Him. I am rooted and grounded in His love, and I am well able to comprehend with all believers what is the width and length and depth and height of His unfailing love. I have been called to know this rich love that surpasses knowledge so that I may be filled with all the fullness of God.

Truly I am the object of His deepest love and affection!

Because I am rooted and grounded in God's love, I am able to love Him well all my days. He is my first love, and I love Him because He first loved me. I love God with all my heart, soul and strength. All that I do, I do for the love of God.

Because I am so loved by God, I love others well. I love them as He has loved me, which proves me to be His own. I am marked by love and for love.

Scripture references used in this decree

Jeremiah 31:3; 1 John 3:1; Ephesians 1:6; Romans 8:38–39; 1 Corinthians 13:4, 7–8; John 3:16; Hebrews 8:10; Song of Solomon 2:4; 1:2, 4; Ephesians 3:17; 1:18–19; 1 John 4:19; Deuteronomy 6:5; 1 John 4:11; John 13:35

six

Identified with Christ

Many are shaken in their walk with the Lord and fail to grow into maturity simply because they do not know who they are in Christ.

As a professional life coach specializing in the area of spiritual growth, I encourage and exhort my clients to meditate on who they are in Christ. This is what I refer to as "core training." I want them to be unwavering in knowing who they are and what they have in Christ. When your core beliefs are solid, then you can successfully run your race in life, prospering in everything you put your mind to.

In the world of sports, athletes in every discipline train in physical core-strengthening exercises. They can then direct focused strength into their extremities from a solid and fortified core. If their core is weak, they will more than likely falter in their competitions. It is the same with our spiritual core. If our spiritual core is strong, we can direct strength with focus into our lives to bring forth fruitfulness. If our spiritual core is weak, we can falter in life.

When we are born again, the Scriptures explain that a new birth has taken place and that we have now become a new creation—old things have passed away and all things have become new (see 2 Corinthians 5:17).

The Word reveals who we are in Christ. It is our mirror, according to the first chapter of James. Gazing into the Word enables us to see who we are. Reading further, we discover that, unless we take that information and act on it, we will forget what we saw and who we are.

> For if anyone is a hearer of the word and not a doer, he is like a man who looks at his natural face in a mirror; for once he has looked at himself and gone away, he has immediately forgotten what kind of person he was. But one who looks intently at the perfect law, the law of liberty, and abides by it, not having become a forgetful hearer but an effectual doer, this man will be blessed in what he does.
>
> James 1:23–25

One of the ways that we act on the Word is by decreeing it verbally. I have discovered that when I decree the truth about who I am in Christ, I am sealing my identity. I hear it through reading and meditation, which results in faith, but I seal it through decreeing: "For with the heart a person believes, resulting in righteousness, and with the mouth he confesses, resulting in salvation" (Romans 10:10).

According to 1 Thessalonians 5:23, you are a three-part being: You are a spirit, you have a soul and you live in a body. When you are born again, your spirit man receives the spirit of Christ and the miracle of rebirth takes place. We see this confirmed through the words of Jesus in John 3:6 when He taught Nicodemus, a religious leader, that when you are born again, your spirit is born again by the Spirit of God. ("That which is born of the flesh is flesh, and that which is born of the Spirit is spirit.")

As a result of this new birth, old things have passed away and all things have become new. You are now Christlike in your spirit—the innermost part of your being. You have His nature, His life, His righteousness, His gifts, His enablements and all that He is, within your spirit man. You cannot try to create this life—it is a gift. You are transformed within your spirit with His gift of eternal life.

Your soul (mind, will and emotions) and your body, however, are not transformed immediately. The Scriptures teach us that the mind needs to be transformed by the Word.

> And do not be conformed to this world, but be transformed by the renewing of your mind, so that you may prove what the will of God is, that which is good and acceptable and perfect.
>
> Romans 12:2

> But we all, with unveiled face, beholding as in a mirror the glory of the Lord, are being transformed into the same image from glory to glory, just as from the Lord, the Spirit.
>
> 2 Corinthians 3:18

My dear friend Dr. Clarice Fluitt teaches that your born-again spirit is the king of your being. The king is to rule. She likens the soul (the mind, the will and the emotions) to being like a queen who is next to the king and who is to submit to him in honor. Within the soul we find the faculty of the will. The soul makes choices. A godly queen will choose to obey and follow the king, while an evil queen will choose against his will and decide to take things into her own hands. In the natural, for a queen to violate the protocol of submission to the king would be a great offense and could be punishable under the law.

We see an example of this in the first chapter of Esther when Queen Vashti refused to respond to the king's command to be brought to his banquet.

The Bible teaches that our carnal nature is at enmity against God and cannot submit (see Romans 8:7) The queen (soul) must be renewed in order to make right choices in honor of the king (spirit).

Dr. Fluitt further describes the flesh as the servant. The servant (body) does what the queen chooses. The body is to carry out the purposes of the king and to manifest his glory, but it takes its orders from the queen. The Bible teaches that it is a shameful thing for a servant to rule in the house of a king (see Proverbs 19:10). Likewise, our flesh with its lusts and desires must not rule our lives.

In other words, your spirit does not need renewing—it is already perfect. Your soul needs to be renewed by the Word, and this is where decrees help tremendously.

A number of years ago, the Lord spoke to me and said, "Patricia, for a season I am going to shut down your ability to feel and sense Me" (functions of the soul). I was shocked and also disappointed. I remember sheepishly saying, "I don't think that's a good idea . . . . is it?" I am one who loves feelings—emotional and physical.

I asked Him why He would want to do that. He answered, "You depend too much on your emotions. If you feel righteous, you believe you are, and if you feel condemned, you let it sway you. If you feel loved, you believe you are, but if you feel rejected, you allow the lie to affect you. I want you to learn to live from your spirit man. Your spirit man is perfect and is defined by the truth of My Word in Christ. In this next season, I am going to teach you to live out of your spirit man *by faith*. You will not feel Me or sense Me for a season. I will give you two keys: Pray in tongues violently every day and decree who you are in Christ every day. These tools will help you to live from your born-again nature."

The Lord said that this was for a "season." My understanding of a season was that one season lasts about three months (four seasons in a year), but I discovered that the Lord's seasons are not timed the same. My "season" lasted for most of a year, and I wrestled terribly. I had never felt so dry and empty. Even though I *felt* dry and empty, the Word taught me something different: that His Word is truth, not my feelings.

It took me a while to really understand what the Lord was doing. I would get up in the morning to obey the first assignment, "to pray in tongues violently each day." It took me a while to grasp the "violent" part, which I discovered in this Scripture: "The kingdom of heaven suffers violence, and the violent take it by force" (Matthew 11:12 NKJV). The problem for me was that violence is an emotion and I could not feel anything. I would force myself to be "violent" as I prayed in tongues and it felt so phony. I complained, "Lord, I feel like I'm faking it." His response was, "You're not faking it; you are 'faithing' it." With that I continued each morning—but I still did not like it. The Word teaches that when you pray in tongues, you are edified (see 1 Corinthians 14:4). As I prayed in tongues, I did not feel edified but I chose to believe I was.

The second part of the assignment was to declare who I was in Christ every day. The issue for me was, once again, that I had no feelings and I could not spontaneously remember who I was in Christ. Based on what feelings I did have during that initial season, I would have said that I felt more like a "wart" on the Body of Christ, but thankfully I was not supposed to believe what I felt. I searched the Scriptures with the use of a Bible concordance, commentaries and dictionaries, and wrote out what I could find about who I was in Christ. Then I decreed those truths over my life each day. "I am the head and not the tail. . . ." But I did not feel a thing. I felt no excitement, no witness, no nothing! I just had to believe that what I was decreeing was the truth and that it was having impact.

During that year, I discovered that no matter how I felt, the truth was the truth. I was not defined by what I felt or thought—I was defined by the Word. By decreeing the truth about who I was in Christ every day, a fortress of identity was formed within my soul. No longer did I default to the lies of the enemy—I got grounded in the truth.

You can too! *Making daily decrees concerning who you are in Christ will transform and strengthen and fortify you.* You are not striving to become like Christ, because you already are like Him in your spirit. Your decrees will help the river of identity flow into your soul and body from your spirit.

The decrees on the next page are the very ones I decreed in that season. As you decree them daily, you will establish a strong core of belief about who you are in Christ.

QUESTIONS TO PONDER

1. Why is knowing who you are in Christ so important? As you have grown in your understanding of who you are in Christ, in what ways have you grown in other areas as a result (personal, relationships, career, spiritual life)?

2. What were some other areas in which your mind experienced renewing through the Word once you came to Christ? Mention any particular Scriptures that had a particular impact on your life.

3. Do your emotions at any given moment conflict with what the Word says about you? Is there an area you particularly struggle with from time to time? What Scriptures do/can you use to confront and align those feelings with the truth?

Identified with Christ

I am a child of God; God is spiritually my Father.	*Romans 8:14–15; Galatians 3:26; 4:6; John 1:12*
I am a new creation in Christ; old things have passed away and all things have become new.	*2 Corinthians 5:17*
I am in Christ.	*Ephesians 1:1–4; Galatians 3:26, 28*
I am an heir with the Father and a joint heir with Christ.	*Galatians 4:6–7; Romans 8:17*

I am reconciled to God and am an ambassador of reconciliation for Him.	*2 Corinthians 5:18–19*
I am God's workmanship, created in Christ for good works.	*Ephesians 2:10*
I am a citizen of heaven.	*Ephesians 2:19; Philippians 3:20*
I am a member of Christ's body.	*1 Corinthians 12:27*
I am united to the Lord and am one spirit with Him.	*1 Corinthians 6:17*
I am the temple of the Holy Spirit.	*1 Corinthians 3:16; 6:19*
I am a friend of Christ.	*John 15:15*
I am a servant of righteousness.	*Romans 6:18*
I am the righteousness of God in Christ.	*2 Corinthians 5:21*
I am enslaved to God.	*Romans 6:22*
I am chosen and ordained by Christ to bear fruit.	*John 15:16*
I am a prisoner of Christ.	*Ephesians 3:1; 4:1*
I am righteous and holy.	*Ephesians 4:24*
I am hidden with Christ in God.	*Colossians 3:3*
I am the salt of the earth.	*Matthew 5:13*
I am the light of the world.	*Matthew 5:14*
I am part of the true vine.	*John 15:1–2*
I am filled with the divine nature of Christ; I escape the corruption that is in the world through lust.	*2 Peter 1:4*
I am an expression of the life of Christ.	*Colossians 3:4*
I am chosen of God, holy and dearly loved.	*Colossians 3:12; 1 Thessalonians 1:4*
I am a child of light.	*1 Thessalonians 5:5*
I am a partaker of a heavenly calling.	*Hebrews 3:1*
I am more than a conqueror through Christ.	*Romans 8:37*

I am a partaker with Christ and I share in His life.   *Hebrews 3:14*

I am one of God's living stones, being built up in Christ as a spiritual house.   *1 Peter 2:5*

I am part of a chosen generation, a royal priesthood, a holy nation.   *1 Peter 2:9*

I am the devil's enemy.   *1 Peter 5:8*

I am born again by the Spirit of God.   *John 3:3–6*

I am an alien and stranger to this world.   *1 Peter 2:11*

I am a child of God who always triumphs in Christ and releases His fragrance in every place.   *2 Corinthians 2:14*

I am seated in heavenly places in Christ.   *Ephesians 2:6*

I am saved by grace.   *Ephesians 2:8*

I am a recipient of every spiritual blessing in the heavenly places in Christ.   *Ephesians 1:3*

I am redeemed by the blood of the Lamb.   *Revelation 5:9*

I am part of the Bride of Christ and am making myself ready for Him.   *Revelation 19:7*

I am a true worshiper who worships the Father in spirit and in truth.   *John 4:24*

seven

Blessing

You were created for blessing. We find this truth right in the beginning of the Bible. The first thing God did after He created human beings was to bless them.

> So God created man in His own image; in the image of God He created him; male and female He created them. *Then God blessed them*, and God said to them, "Be fruitful and multiply; fill the earth and subdue it; have dominion over the fish of the sea, over the birds of the air, and over every living thing that moves on the earth."
>
> Genesis 1:27–28 NKJV (emphasis added)

After the Fall, humankind came under a curse due to the consequence of sin, and yet God continued to bless. As highlighted previously, we saw the Lord giving instruction to His priests to bless His people by having them decree over them:

> "The LORD bless you, and keep you; the LORD make His face shine on you, and be gracious to you; the LORD lift up His countenance

on you, and give you peace." So they shall invoke My name on the sons of Israel, and I then will bless them.

Numbers 6:24–27

We also discover His clear promises to bless, if His people would obey all He commanded them.

"Now it shall be, if you diligently obey the LORD your God, being careful to do all His commandments which I command you today, the LORD your God will set you high above all the nations of the earth. All these blessings will come upon you and overtake you if you obey the LORD your God. . . ."

Deuteronomy 28:1–2

Due to humankind's fallen condition, it was not possible for God's people to obey all the commandments all the time, yet God's heart was still for the human race to be blessed. His plan of redemption included His Son Jesus Christ coming to the earth as a man and fulfilling all the requirements for people to be made right with God and to receive all His blessings.

His blessings are very great indeed: In Ephesians 1:3, we discover that we have been blessed with "every spiritual blessing in the heavenly places in Christ." In 2 Peter 1:3–4 we find that we have been blessed with "everything pertaining to life and to godliness" and that all the promises in the Bible have been granted us.

Yes, God desires each one of us to be blessed in every area of our lives!

Just think about the blessings and benefits that are available to us in Christ. By definition, "to bless" means to invoke divine care and pronounce holy; to endow; protect and preserve; to approve, speak well of or favor; to confer happiness or prosperity upon. The Bible speaks of both blessings and curses, with blessings being the complete opposite of curses.

I was ministering to a young man once who appeared to be cursed in every area of his life: finances, health and relationships. On a regular basis, his possessions got broken or stolen; he was never promoted in his job and was sometimes blamed for things he had not done; he constantly struggled with viruses and immune system failures; his family was in discord; and he had few sustained friendships.

During the course of ministering to him, we discovered some areas of his life that needed repentance and healing. This is important if you want to live a blessed life. Sin will always attract failure and unwanted consequences, and receiving blessings hinges on obedience to God's Word in life. However, even with all of the ministry, blessings were still not manifesting in his life.

Then I had him decree, each day, the promises of God's Word regarding blessings over his life. I also instructed him to *expect* blessings to manifest, as he had grown over the years to expect things to go wrong. Through the decrees, things started to change for him. Doors of opportunity opened, promotion came, his physical body was strengthened with health, new friendships were established and things began to change in his financial status. He saw only small breakthroughs at first, but he noticed a slight shift less than thirty days after beginning his decrees of blessing.

Know that in Christ you are already blessed. This has been settled! You are not trying to "get blessed" by decreeing the Word. But *when you decree God's truth over your life, everything that is not true will move out of the way.* Curses must bow to a decree of the Word of God. Blessings come looking for you at the decree of the Word of God. When you decree

God's Word of blessings over your life, you become a blessing magnet—blessings are attracted to you.

Send forth God's decree of blessing over your life and all that pertains to it, and you *will* be blessed. The Word will not return void but will truly accomplish everything it is sent to do. Send forth decrees of blessing over your loved ones too, and see what happens! Whenever you bless another by decreeing God's Word, they will be blessed, but you will also receive a harvest of blessing back into your life according to the decrees you have sown.

You are blessed to bless! When believers ask me to help them identify their callings, I always suggest that if they do not know specifically what God has called them to, they can begin by engaging in the ministry of blessing. Decreeing blessings over yourself and others will help launch you into that ministry.

QUESTIONS TO PONDER

1. Ephesians 1:3 says that we are blessed "with every spiritual blessing in the heavenly places in Christ." What are some of these spiritual blessings and how have you personally experienced them?

2. Review the various aspects of what it means to bless and be blessed by God. Which of these have you experienced in your life? Protection? Favor? Prosperity? Which

would you like to see more? To increase these manifestations of blessing, look for one or two Scriptures that you can personalize and decree.

_____

_____

_____

3. What are the benefits when you decree blessing over others—both in their lives and in yours? How have you experienced this harvest?

_____

_____

_____

Decree

Blessing

I am created for blessing. As a result, I am fruitful in every good thing, and I multiply and increase in blessing. Because my God has blessed me, no curse can touch me. In the name of Jesus Christ and by the power of His blood, I decree His covenant of blessing around my life and all that pertains to me.

Nothing but blessing is permitted to come into my life or sphere of influence. If the enemy attempts to attack me, he will be caught in the act and pay sevenfold what he stole, and then I will plunder his house, for I only accept blessing. His attempts create testimonies of God's increased blessings in my life.

Like Abraham, I am blessed and am called to be a blessing. Through my life in Jesus, nations are blessed.

Blessings come upon me and overtake me. Blessings are attracted to me. I am a blessing magnet. I am blessed coming in and blessed going out. I am blessed in the city and blessed in the field. The heavens are open over my life and the rain of God's abundant goodness falls on my life, and all that pertains to me. No good thing has He withheld from me. I am blessed in everything I put my hands to.

My household is blessed. My food is blessed. My clothing is blessed. My vehicles are blessed. My business and matters of business are blessed. My children, family and all who labor with me and for me are blessed. My finances are blessed because Jesus established an eternal, unbreakable covenant of blessing for me.

I am blessed with the Kingdom of heaven and its bounty because I recognize my need of God in all things and at all times. I am blessed with comfort when I mourn. I am always blessed with a satisfied heart because I hunger and thirst for righteousness. I am blessed with mercy because I show mercy to others. I am blessed with insights and visitations from God because I am pure in spirit.

I am called a son/daughter of God because I am a peacemaker. When I am persecuted for the sake of righteousness or when people insult me and speak lies about me, I am blessed with heavenly and eternal reward. I am blessed because I hear the Lord's Word and act on it. I am a doer of the Word and not a hearer only.

Because I love wisdom and righteousness, I am blessed and my dwelling is blessed. The blessing of the Lord has made me rich, and He adds no sorrow to it. Because I trust in the Lord, I am blessed. I am blessed with every spiritual blessing in the heavenly places in Christ. Grace and peace are multiplied unto me in the knowledge of Christ.

I have been granted everything that pertains to life and to godliness. I have been given all the magnificent promises in the Word of God. I sow blessings bountifully, and therefore I reap blessings bountifully. I always look for ways I can bless others. I am truly blessed in all things, for my Father in heaven has chosen gladly to give me the Kingdom.

My God blesses me continuously and causes His face to shine upon me. He is gracious unto me and grants me peace.

Scripture references used in this decree

Genesis 1:28; 12:3; Hebrews 9:14–15; Proverbs 6:31; Genesis 12:2; Galatians 3:14; Deuteronomy 28:1–13; Matthew 5:1–11; Luke 11:28; James 1:22; Proverbs 3:13, 33; 10:6, 22; 16:20; Ephesians 1:3; 2 Peter 1:2–4; 2 Corinthians 9:6; Luke 12:32; Numbers 6:22–27

eight

Favor

Favor is so wonderful! I know that all of you have experienced rejection in your life at some point and all of you have experienced a measure of favor—which one do you like best? Favor—right? This is because you were created for favor and your innermost parts cry out for it. Everyone resists rejection because it is an enemy of the favor we were created for, and yet many are constantly plagued by rejection and/or lack of favor.

When you are favored, blessings follow you, doors open for you, promotions are offered you and people like being around you. People who know favor have many friends and everything around them flourishes. This is what God desires for you.

We see that Jesus grew in favor with both God and man when He walked the earth in His human form. "And Jesus kept increasing in wisdom and stature, and in favor with God and men" (Luke 2:52). He desires you to grow in favor also.

The beautiful quality of God's favor toward you is that it is a gift and not earned or warranted. We are favored by God when we believe in and receive His Son. The favor that He declared over His Son at His baptism has been given to us who receive Christ. This is wonderful! Not only is it a free gift, it lasts for a lifetime—there is never a time when God's favor diminishes. You are favored in Christ when you are young, when you are old and everything in between.

Favor is a great weapon to utilize against the enemy of rejection. *You can be set free from rejection simply by decreeing the Word*, and I have seen it happen many times. I remember a little boy named Sammy, who suffered great rejection at school. He had some behavioral issues due to attention deficit disorder. His mother grieved over all that both he and she had to deal with due to the ADD, but the bullying and the rejection he suffered at school was too much for him to bear. He became suicidal at eleven years of age.

I suggested she proclaim decrees of favor over him every day and especially before he went to school. I also suggested she use some visuals of favor decrees and post them on the bathroom mirror and on her fridge. She put some happy photographs of her son engaged in a variety of things he enjoyed on the mirror and fridge, along with some positive affirmations such as "Sammy is loved; Everyone loves Sammy; Sammy is amazing; Sammy is a good person," and so forth.

Every day in her prayer time she would declare a number of favor decrees over Sammy's life, and she also had Sammy decree a few. She wrote out little notes in his lunch bag with decrees of favor on them.

Before the school year was out, everything had changed for Sammy. He had friends; he was happy and ready to face his future. No more rejection.

Sammy was not created to handle rejection, and neither are you. You are created for favor. God wants you to enjoy increased favor all throughout your entire life, and one key to secure this amazing favor is the power in decrees. Use the decree of God's Word that follows to empower *favor* in your life. Enjoy decreeing this daily but especially when you need special favor. You are favored!

QUESTIONS TO PONDER

1. What would "growing in favor with God and men" look like to you personally?

2. Is there someone in your life who is especially needing favor at this time? How can you team up with them, share some of the following decrees of favor and "agree to agree" together to start decreeing these?

3. Can you think of a time when you experienced God's favor in a very special way? How does the knowledge that His favor lasts for a lifetime encourage you?

Favor

In Christ Jesus, I am favored by my heavenly Father. The favor He has given His Son has been given to me. This is undeserved, unmerited favor that is granted me in Christ. His favor is a free gift to me, for which I am very thankful. As Jesus kept increasing in wisdom and stature and in favor with God and men, so also do I, because I abide in Jesus and He abides in me.

I embrace the favor of God, which is better than silver and gold. The favor of God on my life endures for a lifetime and causes my influence and blessing to stand strong. His favor surrounds me like a shield against my enemies.

The Lord favors me with vindication and delights in my prosperity. His blessing on my life attracts prosperous people who seek my favor.

By the favor of the Lord, the works of my hands are confirmed and established. All that I put my hands to is favored. Even as God blessed Job in the days of his prime, my steps also are bathed in butter and the rock pours out oil for me. As I seek the Lord's favor, He is gracious to me according to His Word. I am favored in my home and favored in the workplace. I am favored everywhere I go and in all that I do.

I love wisdom and seek diligently for wisdom and understanding. Therefore I have been granted favor by the Lord and favor by others.

In the light of my King's face is life, and His favor is like a cloud with the spring rain over me. His favor is like heavenly dew that falls on my life.

I am favored in His presence, and He goes before me, revealing His goodness and glory to me. His favor opens doors of opportunity for me that no man can shut. By His favor I have been granted the keys of the Kingdom, and whatever I bind on earth is bound in heaven. Whatever I loose on earth has been loosed in heaven. His righteous scepter of favor is extended toward me.

Whatever I ask in the name of Christ He grants unto me when I make my requests and petitions according to His will. He daily grants me great favor because of the covenant blood of Christ and the promises in His Word.

Blessed be the Lord who favors His people!

Scripture references used in this decree

John 17:22; Ephesians 2:8–9; Luke 2:52; Proverbs 22:1; Psalm 30:5, 7; Psalm 5:12; Psalm 35:27; Psalm 45:12; Psalm 90:17; Job 29:6; Psalm 119:58; Deuteronomy 28:4–6; Proverbs 8:35; 11:27; Proverbs 16:15; 19:12; Exodus 33:13–19; Isaiah 45:1; Matthew 16:19; Psalm 45:6; Esther 5:2; John 15:7; Ephesians 1:3, 7 *nine*

Victory

You will not get through life without facing obstacles and resistance, along with seasons of spiritual, relational and circumstantial attacks. Everyone has their battle stories. Jesus ensured us that as long as we were in the world, we would have tribulation (see John 16:33). We are taught through the writings of Peter that the devil prowls around "like a roaring lion, seeking someone to devour" (1 Peter 5:8). Paul exhorted us to wear the full armor of God so that we would withstand the schemes of the evil one (see Ephesians 6:11). Jesus gave us insight into the very nature of the devil by telling us that he came to "steal and kill and destroy" (John 10:10). So the question is not *if* we are going to face battles in life, for we surely will. The question is, "*How* will we position ourselves in the midst of them?"

The Word clearly reveals that, as we align ourselves with God, we will win every battle:

But thanks be to God, who *always leads us in triumph in Christ*, and manifests through us the sweet aroma of the knowledge of Him in every place.

> 2 Corinthians 2:14 (emphasis added)

"No weapon that is formed against you will prosper; and every tongue that accuses you in judgment you will condemn. This is the heritage of the servants of the LORD, and their vindication is from Me," declares the LORD.

> Isaiah 54:17

Who shall separate us from the love of Christ? Shall tribulation, or distress, or persecution, or famine, or nakedness, or peril, or sword? As it is written: "For Your sake we are killed all day long; we are accounted as sheep for the slaughter." Yet in all these things we are more than conquerors through Him who loved us.

> Romans 8:35–37 NKJV

As believers in Christ, we have been given Christ's victory! Jesus won the battle over sin, death and the grave. He is the powerful conqueror! He gave us His authority to "tread on serpents and scorpions, and over all the power of the enemy" (Luke 10:19).

Some of the challenges you might face in life could include assaults on your peace, finances and provision, health, relationships, spirituality and fruitfulness. However difficult these attacks might be, *every assault you encounter is an invitation to experience Christ's victory—and you can decree it!*

Our mission's leader had discovered some serious "foul play" in one of the local ministries in the nation we were serving. The foul play involved proven exploitation of the children who were in their care. When she confronted it, all hell broke out against her. There was not a day when she did not face verbal assaults that attempted to discredit her, and she even received threats on her life. The spiritual oppression was severe. She then began to encounter conflicts within her team as the warfare escalated over a period of a year. We walked through that season anchored in the unwavering understanding that Jesus' victory was secure over her and all that pertained to her and our mission there. Even though there were daily battles, we locked in to the truth of God's Word.

Our intercessors undergirded our team leader and the mission assignment with decrees of victory. They "sent forth" the Word to demolish the strongholds of the enemy and to protect our leader and her laborers. She herself was also tenacious in prayer and standing on the promises.

Victory came in waves over that year. There was retaliation along with the evidences of breakthrough. Finally after a year of intense battle, everything settled and the ministry went to a new level of operative anointing, authority in the Spirit and fruitfulness.

I love the encouragement Peter gives us to help during times of trial:

> Be sober, be vigilant; because your adversary the devil walks about like a roaring lion, seeking whom he may devour. Resist him, steadfast in the faith, knowing that the same sufferings are experienced by your brotherhood in the world. But may the God of all grace, who called us to His eternal glory by Christ Jesus, after you have suffered a while, perfect, establish, strengthen, and settle you.
>
> 1 Peter 5:8–10 NKJV

As you are reading this chapter, you might be thinking, "That's me! I have been bombarded by the enemy!" If this is so, then you can start to rejoice right now! You are going to have a serious testimony of your breakthrough, and it *will* come! I realize that it probably does not feel like your trial is a blessing at this time, but look at what James teaches us:

> My brethren, count it all joy when you fall into various trials, knowing that the testing of your faith produces patience. But let patience have its perfect work, that you may be perfect and complete, lacking nothing.
>
> James 1:2–4 NKJV

When you come through to the other side of the battle you are facing, you will be perfected and matured, lacking in nothing. What a promise!

QUESTIONS TO PONDER

1. What is a particular area/situation in which God has "led you into triumph"? What are some Scriptures that encouraged you during this time?

_____

_____

_____

2. Is there an area in which you and/or a loved one are needing to experience victory at this time? How will the following decrees turn things around?

_____

_____

_____

3. Why should we count it "all joy" when we fall into trials? How have trials caused you to grow personally?

Decree

Victory

I am a child of the living God. I am an heir of God and a joint heir with Jesus Christ. I am a new creation in Jesus and old things have passed away and all things have become new. I am part of a chosen generation, a royal priesthood, a holy nation.

I am not under guilt or condemnation. I refuse discouragement because it is not of God. God is the God of all encouragement. There is therefore now no condemnation for those who are in Christ Jesus. The law of the Spirit of life in Christ Jesus has set me free from the law of sin and death. I do not listen to Satan's accusations, for he is a liar, the father of lies. I gird up my loins with truth. Sin does not have dominion over me.

I flee from temptation, but if I do sin, I have an advocate with the Father, who is Jesus Christ. I confess my sins and forsake them. God is faithful and just to forgive me, cleansing me from all unrighteousness. I am cleansed by the blood of the Lamb. I am an overcomer because of the blood of Jesus and because of the word of my testimony.

No weapon that is formed against me shall prosper, and I shall confute every tongue that rises up against me in judgment. My mind is renewed by the Word of God.

The weapons of my warfare are not carnal but mighty through God to the pulling down of strongholds; I cast down imaginations and every high thing that exalts itself against the knowledge of Christ. I bring every thought captive into obedience to the truth.

I am accepted in the Beloved. Greater is He that is in me than he that is in the world. Nothing can separate me from the love of God which is in Christ Jesus my Lord. I am the righteousness of God in Christ Jesus. I am not a slave of sin, but rather of righteousness. I continue in His Word. I know the truth, and the truth sets me free. Because Christ has set me free, I am free indeed. I have been delivered out of the domain of darkness and am now abiding in the Kingdom of God.

I am not intimidated by the enemy's lies. He is defeated. For this purpose Christ came into the world, to destroy the works of the evil one. I submit to God and resist the devil. The enemy flees from me in terror because the Lord lives mightily in me. I give the devil no opportunity. I give no place to fear in my life. God has not given me a spirit of fear but of love, of power and of a sound mind. Terror shall not come near me because the Lord is the strength of my life and He always causes me to triumph in Christ Jesus.

In Christ, I am the head and not the tail. I am above and not beneath. A thousand shall fall at my side and ten thousand at my right hand and none shall touch me. I am seated with Christ in the heavenly places far above all principalities and powers. I have been given power to tread upon serpents, scorpions and over all the power of the enemy. Nothing shall injure me. No longer will the enemy oppress me. I defeat him by the authority that Christ has given me. I am more than a conqueror through Christ.

Scripture references used in this decree

Romans 8:16–17; 2 Corinthians 5:17; 1 Peter 2:9; Romans 8:1–2; John 8:44; Ephesians 6:14; Romans 6:14; 1 John 2:1; 1 John 1:9 ; Revelation 7:14; Revelation 12:11; Isaiah 54:17; Romans 12:1; 2 Corinthians 10:3–5; Ephesians 1:6; 1 John 4:4; Romans 8:39; 2 Corinthians 5:21; Romans 6:18; John 8:32, 36; Colossians 1:13; John 3:8; James 4:7; Ephesians 4:27; 2 Timothy 1:7; 2 Corinthians 2:14; Psalm 27:1; Deuteronomy 28:13; Psalm 91:7; Luke 10:19; Romans 8:37

ten

Wisdom

Wisdom is the ability to perceive and understand situations from God's perspective and to implement choices and actions according to His Word. Wisdom will protect you from making unhealthy choices that bring about unwanted or devastating consequences and will cause you to be blessed as you walk on God's ordained path for your lives.

In Proverbs 4:7, we discover that wisdom is "the principal thing": "Wisdom is the principal thing; therefore get wisdom" (NKJV). In other words, wisdom is supremely important, the most important thing to have in your life. Seek wisdom above all else, and every area of your life will improve.

The following are some valuable benefits of wisdom:

1. Wisdom keeps you from pride, arrogance and the evil way.

> "I, wisdom, dwell with prudence, and find out knowledge and discretion. The fear of the LORD is to hate evil; pride

and arrogance and the evil way and the perverse mouth
I hate."

Proverbs 8:12–13 NKJV

2. Wisdom grants understanding, counsel and strength.

"Counsel is mine, and sound wisdom; I am understanding, I have strength."

Proverbs 8:14 NKJV

3. Wisdom gives sound insight to leaders and empowers them to rule.

"By me kings reign, and rulers decree justice. By me princes
rule, and nobles, all the judges of the earth."

Proverbs 8:15–16 NKJV

4. Wisdom protects you from stumbling, from fear and sudden terror.

My child, never drift off course from these two goals for
your life: to walk in wisdom and to discover discernment. Don't ever forget how they empower you. . . .
They give you living hope to guide you, and not one
of life's tests will cause you to stumble. You will sleep
like a baby, safe and sound—your rest will be sweet and
secure. You will not be subject to terror, for it will not
terrify you. Nor will the disrespectful be able to push you
aside.

Proverbs 3:21, 23–25 TPT

5. Wisdom gives you a blueprint for life.

The Lord laid the earth's foundations with wisdom's
blueprints. By his living-understanding all the universe
came into being.

Proverbs 3:19 TPT

6. Wisdom builds strong homes and healthy family relationships.

By wisdom a house is built, and by understanding it is established.

Proverbs 24:3

7. Wisdom attracts favor in your life.

"For he who finds me finds life and obtains favor from the LORD."

Proverbs 8:35

The king's favor is toward a servant who acts wisely, but his anger is toward him who acts shamefully.

Proverbs 14:35

8. Wisdom enables you to be victorious in life battles.

A wise man scales the city of the mighty and brings down the stronghold in which they trust.

Proverbs 21:22

For by wise guidance you will wage war, and in abundance of counselors there is victory.

Proverbs 24:6

9. Wisdom helps you succeed.

Using a dull ax requires great strength, so sharpen the blade. That's the value of wisdom; it helps you succeed.

Ecclesiastes 10:10 NLT

10. Wisdom leads in paths of righteousness and justice.

"I walk in the way of righteousness, in the midst of the paths of justice."

Proverbs 8:20

11. Wisdom promotes you.

> Exalt her, and she will promote you; she will bring you honor, when you embrace her.
>
> Proverbs 4:8 NKJV

> The wise shall inherit glory, but shame shall be the legacy of fools.
>
> Proverbs 3:35 NKJV

12. Wisdom grants you long life.

> Long life is in her right hand; in her left hand are riches and honor.
>
> Proverbs 3:16

13. Wisdom provides you with riches and honor.

> "Riches and honor are with me, enduring riches and righteousness."
>
> Proverbs 8:18 NKJV

> "To endow those who love me with wealth, that I may fill their treasuries."
>
> Proverbs 8:21

14. Wisdom appeases wrath.

> Scoffers set a city aflame, but wise men turn away wrath.
>
> Proverbs 29:8 NKJV

15. Wisdom brings health and healing.

> Do not be wise in your own eyes; fear the LORD and depart from evil. It will be health to your flesh, and strength to your bones.
>
> Proverbs 3:7–8 NKJV

The Scriptures teach us how to secure wisdom in our lives.

1. If you seek wisdom, you will find wisdom (see Proverbs 8:17).
2. If you love wisdom, wisdom will love you (see Proverbs 8:17).
3. If you pray for wisdom in faith without doubting, you will receive wisdom (see James 1:5, 6).

Wisdom is one of the greatest and most valuable pursuits in any individual's life. When I was awakened to this revelation in the early 1980s, I read through the first eight to ten chapters of the book of Proverbs every day, and I decreed with faith the promises concerning wisdom over my life. For years, this was my routine every morning. Over time, I gained equity in the area of wisdom and I discovered that even at times when I was not directly seeking it, wisdom from God would flood my understanding.

I remember one situation, when I was counseling a couple who was having severe marriage challenges. I listened carefully to each of them. Their perspectives were completely different from each other, and there was great tension and animosity between them. I recall being confused about how to minister to them when suddenly a specific word of wisdom came into my heart for them that turned out to be the very key to their breakthrough. That word of wisdom entered my heart without me seeking directly for it at that moment. The decrees of God's Word and my focus on wisdom over the previous months had created a landing strip for His wisdom to light right when I needed it.

I have seen God's wisdom grant solutions to problems, insights that settle confusion, direction into the unknown and peace in the midst of turmoil. Wisdom is a wonderful gift that is offered to everyone who believes.

When you regularly decree God's Word regarding wisdom, your life will be filled with it. The Word you decree will not return empty but will fill you with wisdom. Daily decrees of wisdom will bring great benefit to your life.

QUESTIONS TO PONDER

1. Mention two benefits of wisdom that you have experienced personally, and how.

2. The Word tells us that when we lack wisdom, we should ask God for it. Is there a particular area or situation for which you are seeking His divine wisdom? How will you implement decrees (such as the following one) in your daily search?

3. On the next page, look over the Scripture-based decree on wisdom. Which portions particularly encourage you, and why?

Wisdom

Jesus Christ has become wisdom, righteousness, sanctification and redemption to me. Because Christ dwells within me, I know wisdom and instruction. My God gives me a spirit of wisdom and of revelation in the knowledge of Christ. When I lack wisdom, I ask in faith, and it is given to me generously. This is heavenly wisdom, which is first pure, then peaceable, gentle, easily entreated, full of mercy and good fruits, unwavering and without hypocrisy.

I discern the sayings of understanding, and I receive instruction in wise behavior, justice and fairness. I walk in the fear of the Lord, which is the beginning of knowledge. Jesus pours out His spirit of wisdom upon me and makes His words of wisdom known to me.

I receive the sayings of wisdom, and I treasure the commandments of the Lord within me. My ear is attentive to wisdom and I incline my heart to understanding. I cry for discernment and lift my voice for understanding.

I seek for wisdom as for silver and search for it as for hidden treasures. Because of this I will discern the fear of the Lord and discover the knowledge of God. The Lord gives me wisdom.

From His mouth come knowledge and understanding. He stores up sound wisdom for me. He is a shield to me. He guards my paths with justice and preserves my way. Wisdom enters my heart, and knowledge is pleasant to my soul. Discretion guards me, and understanding watches over me to deliver me from the way of evil.

I do not let kindness and truth leave me. I bind them around my neck and write them on the tablet of my heart so that I find favor and good repute with God and man. I trust in the Lord with all my heart, and I do not lean on my own understanding. In all my ways I acknowledge Him, and He makes my paths straight. I am blessed because I find wisdom and I gain understanding.

I have a long, full life because it is in wisdom's right hand, and I have the riches and honor that are in wisdom's left hand. Because I love wisdom, all my paths are peace and my ways pleasant. Wisdom is a tree of life to me, and I am blessed because I hold her fast. I inherit honor because of my love for wisdom, and my dwelling is blessed.

I acquire wisdom and understanding. I do not forsake wisdom; therefore, wisdom is my guard. I love wisdom and am watched over. Because I prize and embrace wisdom, wisdom exalts and honors me. Wisdom places a garland of grace on my head and presents me with a crown of beauty. I call wisdom my sister and understanding my intimate friend.

Because I love wisdom, both riches and honor are with me, enduring wealth and righteousness. Wisdom bestows a rich inheritance on me. I listen to wisdom and daily watch at her gates. I eat wisdom's food and drink of the wine that she has mixed. I forsake folly and live. I proceed in the way of understanding. When I speak, I speak noble things, and the opening of my mouth produces right things. My mouth utters truth. All the utterances of my mouth are in righteousness because I walk in the way of wisdom.

Scripture references used in this decree

1 Corinthians 1:30; Ephesians 1:17; James 1:5; 3:17; Proverbs 1:2–3, 7, 23; 2:1–12; 3:16–18, 33–35; 4:5–9; 7:4; 3:16; 8:21, 34–35; 9:5–6; 8:6–8

eleven

Provision

I love to see God's people blessed with abundant provision, and over the years I have enjoyed the pleasure of helping many come into their provisional victories. Yet I know that many struggle to have enough to meet their needs.

In my experiences working with people who need a breakthrough in this regard, I have discovered four main obstacles many of them face that hinder their prosperity:

1. A mindset that resists the truth regarding God's desire for all His children to live a life filled with abundance and overflow
2. Mismanagement of their resources
3. Lack of obedience to God's instruction in His Word regarding "Kingdom economy"
4. Lack of faith to secure the promises

One of the greatest tools to overcoming all four of these obstacles is Word decrees pertaining to personal provision. As you decree the Word, you will hear yourself declare the truth about God's intentions and promises. As you hear yourself declare the Word, you will renew your mind (see Romans 12:2) and create faith (see Romans 10:17). You will also become aware of the conditions that apply to living in a realm of abundance, and this will help you to obey and steward the provision that God entrusts you with.

In the first chapter of this book, I shared with you my experience of learning to live by faith in the area of provision. It took a five-year battle before we could secure our breakthrough, but every day we decreed promises in the Word of God concerning our finances and resources. We did not realize it at the time, but we were building massive equity in the Spirit, so that when we finally secured the breakthrough, realms of abundance manifested in every area of our lives and ministry. We are enjoying the victory of that season to this very day. The most significant key to our breakthrough into a sustained realm of prosperity was making daily decrees of His promises.

I prepared an audio file called Decrees for Kids, and one of the decrees was about provision. The goal of the project was to decree into a child's heart and mind the power of God's truth covering many areas of the child's life. Now at events, mothers and their children often approach me to share how the decrees made a difference in their lives.

One testimony that touched my heart in particular regards a little boy who began to listen to the decrees every night at age nine. When he was eleven, he became an entrepreneur and prospered in his little business endeavor. His mother attributed both his creativity and the resulting financial success to those decrees that had filled his mind and heart every night.

Nowhere in the Bible will you find God promising you lack or poverty. The Word promises us abundance! He wants all His children to prosper on earth, as it is in heaven! I have seen so many turnarounds in people's lives when they have become intentional and faithful about declaring daily decrees regarding their material provision.

One young gal I mentored had come from a very broken and dysfunctional family background. The family was very poor, to the point where often the children lacked food to eat; they lived in a run-down room in the inner city. She did not have good role models, and she was never taught proper stewardship in the area of finances.

When I began working with her, I taught her the biblical principles of tithing, giving to the poor and sowing and reaping financial seed. She went for it! I also taught her to declare Word decrees for financial prosperity. Within the first month she was already seeing breakthroughs, and within two years she was greatly prospering.

I have seen this over and over. *When you make Word decrees, you are building a framework in the spirit realm that God will fill*: "By faith we understand that the worlds were prepared by the word of God" (Hebrews 11:3).

God has given you the power to make wealth (see Deuteronomy 8:18). Word decrees bring forth wealth.

We are not supposed to love the world and its materialistic emphasis, and neither are we to love money; after all, "the love of money is the root of all evil" (1 Timothy 6:10 KJV). Our hearts always need to exalt God above all else, but as we do so, all the "things" get added to us (see Matthew 6:33). God wants you blessed beyond measure!

QUESTIONS TO PONDER

1. Have you struggled to truly believe that God wants you
   (and all His children) to prosper? If so, what was the
   source of that struggle? What are some Scriptures that
   can help counter this false belief?

2. How do tithing, sowing and giving to the needy con-
   tribute to your prosperity? Give a testimony of God's
   faithfulness in your own life in this regard.

3. Do you struggle financially? Review the four obstacles
   mentioned in the devotion. Do you recognize any of
   these as a pattern in your own life? How will decreeing
   the Word help?

Decree

Provision

I seek first the Kingdom of God and His righteousness, and all the things that I need are added unto me, for my heavenly Father knows what I need even before I ask. I do not fear, for it is my Father's good pleasure to give me the Kingdom.

I acknowledge that all my needs are met by Christ Jesus according to God's riches in glory. Grace and peace are multiplied to me through the knowledge of God and of Jesus my Lord. His divine power has given me all things that pertain to life and godliness, through the knowledge of the One who has called me to glory and virtue. Blessed be the God and Father of my Lord Jesus Christ, who has blessed me with every spiritual blessing in the heavenly places in Christ. The Lord is a sun and a shield to me and will give me grace and glory. No good thing will He withhold from me as I walk uprightly.

I choose to sow bountifully; therefore I will reap bountifully. I give to the Lord, to His people and to the needy as I purpose in my heart to give. I do not give grudgingly or out of compulsion, for my God loves a cheerful giver. God makes all grace abound toward me. I always have enough for all things so that I may abound in every good work.

The Lord supplies seed for me to sow and bread for my food. He also supplies and multiplies my seed for sowing, and He increases the fruits of my righteousness. I am enriched to a great degree so that I can continue to be abundantly generous, which increases the thanksgiving to God among those who receive what I share with them.

I bring all my tithes into the Lord's storehouse so that there is provision in His house. As a result, He opens up the windows of heaven and pours out so much blessing for me that there is not room enough to contain it. He rebukes the devourer for my sake, preserving the abundance He has given me.

People everywhere shall call me blessed, for I shall have a delightful life. I am blessed because I consider the poor. Because I give freely to the poor, I will never want. My righteousness endures forever.

I remember the Lord my God, for it is He who gives me the power to make wealth, that He may confirm His covenant. Because Jesus Christ, my Savior, diligently listened to the voice of God and obeyed all the commandments, the Lord has set Him high above all the nations of the earth. Christ became poor so that through His poverty I might become rich. With Him and because of Him, all the blessings in the Kingdom shall come upon me and overtake me.

Jesus came so that I would have life in its abundance. I am very blessed and favored of God and have been called to be a blessing to others.

Scripture references used in this decree

Matthew 6:32–33; Luke 12:32; Philippians 4:19; 2 Peter 1:2–3; Ephesians 1:3; Psalm 84:11; 2 Corinthians 9:6–11; Malachi 3:10–12; Psalm 41:1; Proverbs 28:27; Psalm 112:9; Deuteronomy 8:18; 28:1–2; 2 Corinthians 8:9; John 10:10; Genesis 12:2

twelve

Godly Character

In a world that is full of corruption, immorality, hatred and violence, it is vital that God's people manifest righteous character. There have been many gifted individuals over the ages who could move mountains with their faith, prophesy with precision, preach with eloquence, give generously and work noteworthy miracles, whose characters, unfortunately, were majorly flawed. In my lifetime, I have seen many of "the mighty" in Christian ministry fall into fornication, adultery, pornography, homosexuality, addictions, bitterness, offense, unforgiveness, pride, lies and love of money. It is always a sad day when we see this happen. The world needs to know we belong to Christ because of our character and not only through demonstrations of His power and gifts.

Imagine a world filled with Christians who are known for their uncompromised, impeccable character—what a wonderful vision! The standard must be raised—and it can be.

The very nature of Christ lives within the spirit of every believer. His nature is perfect in love and flawless in character. Believers can manifest that glorious nature through the exercise of their faith. When we study the Word, it is like looking in a mirror* as it reveals who we are in Christ and all that we have in Him—and we become what we gaze upon. Often in Scripture we find God instructing His people to "look" because if they see it, they can have it—or "be it."

God told Abraham to *lift up his eyes and look* as far as he could to the north, the south, the east and the west because all the land he could see, the Lord was giving to him:

> And the LORD said to Abram, after Lot had separated from him: "Lift your eyes now and look from the place where you are—northward, southward, eastward, and westward; for all the land which you see I give to you and your descendants forever."
>
> Genesis 13:14–15 NKJV

It is important to see through God's perspective. Then we can be sure that what we gaze upon is truly what He desires for us.

We see the principle of becoming what we gaze upon in the story of Jacob claiming the spotted and speckled sheep as his wage when he was ready to separate from Laban. In order to increase the number of such sheep, he prepared rods that were peeled to create a striped, speckled and spotted effect. He placed the rods in the watering troughs so that when the flocks came to drink, they would gaze upon the rods. When the flocks conceived before the rods, their offspring were streaked, speckled and spotted. They reproduced what they gazed upon.

---

*"But we all, with unveiled face, beholding as in a mirror the glory of the Lord, are being transformed into the same image from glory to glory, just as by the Spirit of the Lord" (2 Corinthians 3:18 NKJV).

Now Jacob took for himself rods of green poplar and of the almond and chestnut trees, peeled white strips in them, and exposed the white which was in the rods. And the rods which he had peeled, he set before the flocks in the gutters, in the watering troughs where the flocks came to drink, so that they should conceive when they came to drink. So the flocks conceived before the rods, and the flocks brought forth streaked, speckled, and spotted.

Genesis 30:37–39 NKJV

Water in Scripture (the watering troughs, in this case) often symbolizes the Word. Gazing upon the truth in the Word will transform us, and we will manifest what we see.

I once was helping a young man overcome a pornography addiction. He had struggled since his early teens, and he was now in his twenties. The addiction tormented him. He shared how he had fasted for forty days a number of times over the years, prayed regularly, received inner healing and deliverance and sincerely attempted with all his strength to resist the ferocious temptations. He was desperate for breakthrough. As I listened to him share, I noticed over and over he would refer to "his addiction" and to his failures as a Christian. He was locked into shame and guilt and saw himself as a terrible sinner not worthy of the love of God.

I suggested to him that perhaps he was looking in the wrong mirror. I explained that if he continued to look into a mirror in his mind where he saw himself as a completely unworthy, addicted sinner, then that is what he would continue to be, since a person becomes what he gazes upon. I suggested to him that we break that mirror and replace it with a new one that would reflect the nature of God. I began to decree over him who he is in Christ—a righteous, Christ-natured, beloved son of God who is filled with light and who reflects light everywhere he goes.

We went through a prayer of repentance and renunciation and bound the spirit of pornography, serving it an eviction notice in Jesus' name. I asked him, "Do you believe you are free?"

He hesitated and said, "I am not sure."

I explained to him that if a person does not believe, then there is no exchange, that on the cross, Jesus became his sin and gave him His righteousness: "For He made Him who knew no sin to be sin for us, that we might become the righteousness of God in Him" (2 Corinthians 5:21 NKJV). I told him that you cannot work to earn this; rather, it is a gift that you must receive by faith. The fact is that if you believe, sin then loses its power in your life and righteousness manifests in your character.

I sent him home with an assignment: "Look *only* into the right mirror every day, and decree the Word over your life that reveals your godly character." I exhorted him not to give any attention to the devil's lies but to make a commitment to embracing the truth.

And it worked! I have seen him and many others set free by decrees of righteous, godly character. God's Word is true: "You will know the truth and the truth will make you free" (John 8:32).

Whatever you focus on, you empower. If you focus on the devil's lies and your frailties, you will empower them, so do not do that. Instead, focus on the truth. *Decreeing the Word every day will empower Christ's nature in you!* The Word will define you and set you free.

QUESTIONS TO PONDER

1. What character traits does the world need to see in us as Christians? If we all exhibited them, how would it impact the world?

2. How can we compare the Word with a mirror? Has the Word been your mirror? Why or why not?

3. Do you recognize that you sometimes deal with personal character traits that are less than godly? By faith, what transformations are you expecting to take place by habitually decreeing the Word?

Godly Character

I am the light of the world. A city set on a hill cannot be hid. I let my light so shine before men that they may see my good works and glorify my Father which is in heaven. Sin does not have dominion over me because Christ became sin for me and gave me His righteousness. His righteous nature is reflected in and through my character in every area of life.

Grace and peace are multiplied to me through the knowledge of God and of Jesus my Lord. His divine power has granted me everything that pertains to life and to godliness.

He has given me exceeding great and precious promises. I live by these promises so that I might be a partaker of His divine nature, having escaped the corruption that is in the world through lust. Besides this, I diligently add to my faith virtue, and to virtue knowledge, and to knowledge temperance, and to temperance patience, and to patience godliness. To godliness I add brotherly kindness, and to brotherly kindness love. As these things are in me and abounding, I shall never be barren nor unfruitful in the knowledge of my Lord Jesus.

I choose to walk worthy of the Lord in every respect, being fruitful in every good work and increasing in the knowledge of God. I give thanks to my heavenly Father who has made me to be a partaker of the inheritance of the saints in light. He has delivered me from the power of darkness and has translated me to the Kingdom of His dear Son in whom I have redemption through His blood, even the forgiveness of sin.

As a dear child, I am an imitator of God. I walk in love. Therefore fornication, all uncleanness and covetousness have no part in my life, and neither does filthiness or coarse jesting, nor foolish talking. Giving thanks to God, I let no corrupt communication proceed out of my mouth, but only that which is good for edifying, that it may minister grace to the hearers. I will not grieve the Holy Spirit of God, by whom I have been sealed until the day of redemption.

I choose to walk in lowliness of mind and to esteem others as better than myself. I look not to my own interests but also to the interests of others. I make myself of no reputation and take on the role of a bond servant.

I wait for the Lord in all things, and integrity and uprightness preserve me. Jesus is my protection because I walk uprightly. I dwell on those things that are true and honorable—whatever is right, whatever is pure, whatever is lovely, whatever is of good repute and anything that is excellent and worthy of praise.

As a child of God, I am thoroughly equipped for every good work. I consider how to encourage others to love. I put on a heart of compassion, kindness, humility, gentleness and patience. I am God's workmanship, created in Christ Jesus for good deeds, which God prepared beforehand that I should walk in them.

I am patient and kind. I am not jealous. I do not brag, and I am not arrogant. I do not act unbecomingly and do not seek my own way. I am not easily provoked and do not take into account a wrong suffered. I do not rejoice in unrighteousness, but instead I rejoice with the truth. I bear all things, believe all things, hope all things and endure all things. The love of Jesus in me does not fail.

Scripture references used in this decree

Matthew 5:14–16; Romans 6:14; 2 Corinthians 5:21; 2 Peter 1:2–8; Colossians 1:9–14; Ephesians 5:1–5; 4:29–30; Philippians 2:3–7; Proverbs 2:7; Philippians 4:8; 2 Timothy 3:17; Hebrews 10:24; Colossians 3:12; Ephesians 2:10; 1 Corinthians 13:4–8

thirteen

Health and Healing

It is God's will for all people to be healthy and whole in spirit, soul and body. He created the human race without defect, but when sin made its entrance, so also did vulnerability to sickness, disease, injury and accident. Then Jesus came. When He came into the world, He said, "The thief comes only to steal and kill and destroy; I came that they may have life, and have it abundantly" (John 10:10). In 1 John 3:8, we further discover that Jesus came to destroy the works of the evil one—including sickness, disease and attacks of injury, accident and oppression.

I have heard people say that sometimes God makes people sick so that they will draw closer to Him, or in order to teach them a lesson. It is true that when you are sick, you will often draw close to your Comforter and Healer, and you might even learn some good lessons, because He will work everything together for your good (see Romans 8:28). But that does not mean God instigated your sickness. That would be cruel, and our God is a loving God.

Once when my oldest son was a toddler, he ran out in front of a car. I screamed when I saw him headed toward the road, and I ran fast enough to grab him before he got hit. Of course I scolded him and tried to teach him why he should not run out in front of cars, but if I had chosen to teach him that lesson by standing at the roadside waiting for a car to come by so I could throw him out in front of it, that would have been child abuse. For sure he might not ever have had an opportunity to do that again depending on the scope of his injuries, but it would not have been an effective or righteous way to teach him. In this sense, when we hear people say that God gave them cancer or a terrible disease to teach them a lesson, we conclude that they believe He is a child abuser—which He is not!

Jesus taught us to pray for God's will to be done on earth as it is in heaven. Since sickness, disease, injuries or accidents do not exist in heaven, we know we can pray to be free from these things on the earth. Jesus gave clear instruction on how to pray: "Your kingdom come. Your will be done, on earth as it is in heaven" (Matthew 6:10).

On the cross two thousand years ago, Jesus took our sicknesses and torments. Examine the following Scripture:

> Yet he was the one who carried our sicknesses and endured the torment of our sufferings. We viewed him as one who was being punished for something he himself had done, as one who was struck down by God and brought low. But it was because of our rebellious deeds that he was pierced and because of our sins that he was crushed. He endured the punishment that made us completely whole, and in his wounding we found our healing.
>
> Isaiah 53:4–5 TPT

These verses make it clear that Jesus bore our sicknesses, and this is further confirmed in the New Testament when Peter declares, "He Himself bore our sins in His body on the cross, . . . for by His wounds you were healed" (1 Peter 2:24). That means that Jesus took our sicknesses two thousand years ago and in exchange gave us health and healing. We are not waiting to be healed; we already are healed. But we are waiting for the manifestation of the healing, and we connect to His promise by faith.

In the New Testament, we see examples of people exercising their faith to bring healing. One story that I love is the woman with the issue of blood (see Matthew 9:18–26). She pressed in to touch the "hem of Jesus' garment"—this means His tallit or prayer shawl. At the bottom of a prayer shawl are threads tied in knots, with each knot representing a command of God's Word. By seizing the hem of His prayer shawl, she was laying hold of the Word to obtain her healing. Jesus commended her for her faith, which brought her healing instantly.

Let's look at the example of the Roman centurion coming to Jesus on behalf of his servant who was sick. Jesus offered to go to where the servant was, but the centurion had faith that the only action needed was for Jesus to speak a word of healing, even from a distance. The centurion believed in the creative, healing power of Christ's decreed word.

> The centurion answered and said, "Lord, I am not worthy that You should come under my roof. *But only speak a word, and my servant will be healed.* For I also am a man under authority, having soldiers under me. And I say to this one, 'Go,' and he goes; and to another, 'Come,' and he comes; and to my servant, 'Do this,' and he does it."
>
> When Jesus heard it, He marveled, and said to those who followed, "Assuredly, I say to you, I have not found such great faith, not even in Israel!" . . .
>
> Then Jesus said to the centurion, "Go your way; and as you have believed, so let it be done for you." And his servant was healed that same hour.
>
> Matthew 8:8–10, 13 NKJV, emphasis added

As you can see, Jesus made the decree and the servant was healed in that very hour. He sent His Word to heal him.

The Word is that powerful. When you trust it as did the Roman centurion or the woman with the issue of blood, you will see the same results we see in the Bible.

A ministry friend of mine was diagnosed with cancer in her womb. Immediately, we began to decree God's Word over her. She wanted to keep the diagnosis confidential, so I called a few close intercessors who were skilled in decrees and had them take shifts in decreeing the Word. I also played an audio recording by Benny Hinn, "I am the Lord that healeth thee," over her. We were relentless in sending forth the Word by spoken decree and by song. God healed her and she has been cancer-free for years now. The Word works!

When you decree God's Word, you are sending forth His Word to heal but you are also being sustained with health. *Making daily decrees of God's Word will keep you healthy and whole.*

QUESTIONS TO PONDER

1. Based on the Word, what would you tell someone who insists that God sent her a disease to draw her closer to Him?

2. List all that Jesus did on the cross for our benefit:

_____

_____

_____

3. Are you personally dealing with a health issue or do you
   have a loved one or friend who is? Do you firmly believe
   that by decreeing the following decrees, there will be
   breakthrough? Why or why not? If you recognize you
   are still struggling to believe, how, according to what
   you have learned, can you change your beliefs?

_____

_____

_____

Decree

Health and Healing

I praise the Lord with all that is within me and do not forget any of
His benefits. He forgives all my sins and heals all my diseases; He
redeems my life from the pit and crowns me with love and compassion. Jesus satisfies my desires with good things so that my youth is
renewed like the eagle's.

Jesus was wounded for my transgressions. He bore my griefs and
carried away my sicknesses so that I can live in health and wholeness
all my days.

The Lord brings me to health and healing. He heals me and lets
me enjoy abundant peace and security. The Sun of Righteousness

arises for me with healing in His wings, and I go out and leap like a calf released from the stall. Jesus bore my sins in His body on the cross so that I might die to sin and live to righteousness, and therefore the enemy has no power over my body, soul or spirit. By the stripes of Jesus, I am healed. As my days are, so shall my strength be.

Jesus sent forth His Word and healed me; He rescued me from death and the grave. When I cry out, the Lord hears me; He delivers me from all my troubles. The Lord is close to me when I am broken-hearted and saves me when I am crushed in spirit. He sets me free from affliction in body, soul and spirit. He has not given me a spirit of fear that torments my soul, but rather a sound mind. His love and power fill my being.

At times I may have many troubles, but the Lord delivers me from them all. He protects all my bones; not one of them will be broken. I am like an olive tree flourishing in the house of God; I trust in God's unfailing love that grants me health, wholeness and strength forever and ever.

If I get attacked with sickness, I recover when the Lord's people lay hands on me. When I call for the elders to pray over me, anointing me with oil in the name of the Lord, the prayer of faith saves me and the Lord raises me up in wholeness.

The law of the spirit of life in Christ Jesus has set me free from the law of sin and death. Jesus is the resurrection and the life. Because I believe in Him and His resurrection power that lives within me, I will live in divine health and wholeness for all eternity. In Christ I live and move and have my being.

Because I dwell in the shelter of the Most High and rest in the shadow of the Almighty, I will say of the Lord, "He is my refuge and my fortress, my God, in whom I trust." Surely He will save me from the fowler's snare and from the deadly pestilence. He covers me with His feathers, and under His wings I find refuge; His faithfulness is my shield and rampart. I do not fear the terror of night, nor the arrow that flies by day, nor the pestilence that stalks in the darkness, nor the plague that destroys at midday.

Because I make the Most High my dwelling—even the Lord, who is my refuge—then no harm will befall me, no disaster will come near my tent. He will command His angels concerning me, to guard me in all my ways; they will lift me up in their hands, so that I will be protected from injury. Because I love the Lord, He will rescue and protect me from all accident, harm, sickness and disease. With long life He satisfies me and shows me His salvation.

The Lord will sustain me and will restore me to health.

Scripture references used in this decree

Psalm 103:1–3; Isaiah 53:4–5; Jeremiah 33:6; Malachi 4:2; 1 Peter 2:24; Deuteronomy 33:25; Psalm 107:20; Psalm 34:17–19; 2 Timothy 1:7; Psalm 34:19–20; 52:8; James 5:14–15; Romans 8:2; John 11:25–26; Psalm 91; 41:3

fourteen

Spiritual Strength

As mentioned previously, it is my passion and delight to help those I mentor to strengthen their "spiritual core." When they are spiritually aligned to God's truth, every area of their lives is influenced. From a healthy spiritual core, Christ's life and blessings will flow to others and into the world we live in. Jesus said, speaking of the Spirit, that out of our innermost being would flow rivers of living water (see John 7:38–39).

The apostle Paul in his epistles taught about the difference between a believer who is carnal (controlled by fleshly appetites and longings) and one who is spiritual. When the flesh is subdued and the spirit is empowered, blessings manifest. The more in harmony you live with God and His Word, the more every area of your life will be fruitful and productive.

The following are a few Scriptures regarding the carnal nature versus the spiritual nature:

For to be carnally minded is death, but to be spiritually minded is life and peace. Because the carnal mind is enmity against God; for it is not subject to the law of God, nor indeed can be.

Romans 8:6–7 NKJV

And I, brethren, could not speak to you as to spiritual people but as to carnal, as to babes in Christ. . . . for you are still carnal. For where there are envy, strife, and divisions among you, are you not carnal and behaving like mere men? For when one says, "I am of Paul," and another, "I am of Apollos," are you not carnal?

1 Corinthians 3:1, 3–4 NKJV

For the weapons of our warfare are not carnal but mighty in God for pulling down strongholds.

2 Corinthians 10:4 NKJV

Now the works of the flesh are evident, which are: adultery, fornication, uncleanness, lewdness, idolatry, sorcery, hatred, contentions, jealousies, outbursts of wrath, selfish ambitions, dissensions, heresies, envy, murders, drunkenness, revelries, and the like; of which I tell you beforehand, just as I also told you in time past, that those who practice such things will not inherit the kingdom of God.

But the fruit of the Spirit is love, joy, peace, longsuffering, kindness, goodness, faithfulness, gentleness, self-control. Against such there is no law.

Galatians 5:19–23 NKJV

When I have my first coaching session with clients, I invite them to freely share regarding the things they are struggling with. In almost every situation, I discover that their root problem is that they are not anchored in the truth of who they are in Christ. They find themselves frustrated with life, repeating patterns of failure. They have often attempted to change their situations by applying outward aids, but have found no lasting improvement.

Janice's Story

Janice (not her real name) came to my office to seek help. She was frustrated and had been for many years as she suffered with tormenting fears of failure and rejection. She also was often oppressed by night terrors in her dreams. She had tried nutritional supplements to deal with the constant stress and had engaged in counseling, hypnosis and stress-reducing exercises, but every attempt had failed.

I inquired about her beliefs. She was a Christian, but even though she had prayed for Jesus to come into her heart and forgive her sins, she did not understand that He had secured victory for her over all the power of the enemy through His finished work on the cross. She was led by her emotions rather than God's truth. If she felt rejected, then she believed she was rejected. If she felt like a failure, then she believed she was.

I prayed with her to receive the baptism with the Holy Spirit, because we receive power when we have the Holy Spirit (see Acts 1:8). Following her encounter with the Holy Spirit, I encouraged her to pray in tongues* in order to be edified in the nature of God. Praying in tongues builds us up in our faith and in our spiritual nature.

I evaluated her core beliefs and discovered that she did not have a knowledge of the truth regarding a victory-filled life. I gave her some scriptural teachings to study in order to align her beliefs with God's truth, but her greatest breakthrough came as

*Praying in tongues is one of the nine gifts of the Spirit outlined in 1 Corinthians 12:7–11. It is the ability to pray in a God-given language that is unknown to the one speaking it.

a result of making daily Word decrees that targeted her spiritual core. As the Word went to work in her life, she became more confident, she was able to fight off the lies that bombarded her mind and she began to experience favor and success in her workplace. Nightmares became less frequent, and when she did have one, she was able to achieve stability quickly.

The fact is that the Word declares the truth about who you are and what you have. *The more you decree it, the more strengthened you become.*

Everyone needs to be spiritually strengthened. King David was a mighty king, but there were times he was discouraged and confused. At those times, he "encouraged himself in the LORD" (1 Samuel 30:6 KJV). Once he was spiritually strengthened, he could lead with confidence and success.

You will live a full life, too, when your spiritual core is strengthened. Decrees will help strengthen you.

QUESTIONS TO PONDER

1. What is the difference between being led by one's emotions and being led by God's truth? Are you firmly rooted in the truth? Are there areas where truth is your "default" but other areas where your emotions seem to take the reins?

2. How does praying in tongues strengthen you spiritually? Do you have and practice this gift? If not, ask God for it. We are encouraged to seek "all spiritual gifts" in the Bible. You will be strengthened and built up spiritually, your devotional life and intimacy with Jesus will be greatly enhanced, and much more.

3. Read the Scriptures on which each part of the following decree for spiritual strength is based. (They are listed after the decree.) Do some of them particularly stand out to you? Why? Do they refer to truths where you especially need to build more "spiritual muscle"?

Decree

Spiritual Strength

I am strong in the Lord and in the strength of His might. I put on the full armor of God. In Christ I can do all things, because He strengthens me.

The Lord is my strength and my shield; my heart trusts in Him and I am helped; therefore my heart exults and I thank Him with my song. He is my strength and my saving defense in time of trouble. The grace of the Lord Jesus Christ is with my spirit.

I build myself up in my holy faith, praying in the Holy Spirit. As I do this, I keep myself strong in the love of God. My God keeps me from falling and presents me faultless and blameless in the presence of my heavenly Father with great joy.

My help comes from the Lord who made heaven and earth. He will not allow my foot to slip. The Lord is my keeper, and He who keeps me will never slumber. The Lord shades me; therefore I am protected from the heat of the day and the terrors of the night. The Lord protects me from all evil. He keeps my soul, and He guards my going out and my coming in from this time forth and forever after.

When I pass through the valley of weeping, the Lord makes it like a place of refreshing springs for me. I go from strength to strength in the Lord. He lights my way like the sun, and He shields me in every harmful encounter. He gives me grace and glory, and no good thing does He withhold from me. I am blessed because I trust in Him.

According to the riches of His glory, my heavenly Father grants me the ability to be strengthened with power through His Spirit in my inner man so that, with Christ dwelling in my heart through faith, I, being rooted and grounded in love, may be able to comprehend its breadth and length and height and depth and to know the love of Christ that surpasses knowledge, filled up to all the fullness of God. I do not lose heart in doing good, for in due time I shall reap if I do not lose heart.

My eyes are clear; therefore my whole being is full of light. I am steadfast, immovable, always abounding in the work of the Lord, knowing that my toil is not in vain in the Lord. God is my strong fortress, and He sets my feet on His way.

By Him, I can run through any opposition or leap over any barrier. He is a shield, and I take refuge in Him. He makes me able to climb mountains of difficulty with the sure-footed agility of a deer. He equips me for every battle so that I can prevail over my enemies. I am protected by the shield of His salvation; His help makes me strong enough to pursue my enemies and destroy them.

When I am weary, the Lord gives me strength, and when I lack vigor, He rejuvenates me. By waiting on the Lord, I renew my strength.

I can then soar like an eagle and keep moving forward powerfully, without stopping. He sustains me always.

Scripture references used in this decree

Ephesians 6:10–11; Philippians 4:13; Psalm 28:7–8; 2 Corinthians 13:14; Jude 20–21, 24; Psalm 121:1–8; 84:5–7, 11; Ephesians 3:16–19; Galatians 6:9; Matthew 6:22; 1 Corinthians 15:58; 2 Samuel 22:30–40; Isaiah 40:29–31

fifteen

Family and Children

God is a deeply relational God who longs to pour out love on all His creation. Human beings, however, have a special place in His heart as He made us in His image and likeness. In the very first book of the Bible you will find God initiating family. He blessed Adam and Eve to be fruitful and multiply. A man and his wife were blessed to bring forth children.

The Home and Family is not only the first "mountain of influence"* found in the Bible, but to this day I believe it is the most important realm of influence, although it can also be the most neglected and attacked. When the family is strong, the nation is strong. When the family is broken, the nation is affected negatively.

*The "Seven Mountains of Influence" in society (Home and Family, Religion, Business, Government, Arts and Entertainment, Media, and Education), a major teaching concept emphasized in the 1990s and early 2000s by Lance Wallnau, Loren Cunningham and others, brought awareness to believers about how to influence these spheres within the culture for the advancement of the Kingdom of God.

In our lives we have many meaningful relationships, and every loved one in our lives, whether a family member or a friend or an acquaintance, should be a target for our loving influence. We should cherish and steward all of our relationships. The family exposes us to our first relationships in life, and then as members of God's family in Christ, we have authority to release blessing, protection and covering more broadly through our prayers and decrees.

When we send forth God's Word over our family members, that decree goes to work on their behalf. I have seen numerous breakthroughs in families through daily decrees of the Word. Wayward children have returned to Christ, unsaved spouses have come to the Lord and entire families have been set free from rejection and poverty—all as a result of decrees of the Word.

Here are a few stories to encourage you. (None of the names mentioned below are their real names.)

Harold's Story

Harold had transgressed his marriage covenant through an affair. His wife, devastated, had left him, taking their two sons. Harold had come to his senses, ended the affair, and was sincerely broken and repentant. He was receiving counseling and inner healing for some of the root causes that contributed to the vulnerability, but his wife had made up her mind to file for divorce.

He understood that she had a right to divorce him, but he cried out to God for mercy, and every day he made decrees such as the following:

"I decree in Jesus' name that I am forgiven and that sincere, healing love for my wife and children fills my life and floods their hearts. I decree that God can make all things new and that nothing is impossible for Him. I decree and declare restoration and healing for my family, whether the divorce goes through or not—I desire the best for them."

He decreed this every day, numerous times a day. He felt deeply for all his wife was going through, and he understood that although he did not deserve to have his family back, he could trust in the mercy of God. After ten months of decrees, his wife was visited by the Lord in a powerful encounter. Healing began to take place in her heart through that encounter, following which she began to desire restoration of their marriage. It took some time and some counseling, but within the next six months, they were restored. The children also received healing, and the family was blessed to walk in greater love toward each other than before.

Grace's Story

Grace's daughter was a precious, beautiful girl—a good girl growing up. When she was eighteen, she left home to go to college, where she got involved with parties, alcohol, drugs and sexual activity. When Grace became aware of this, she was crushed. She confronted her daughter but could not get through to her. In fact, her daughter had become rebellious and resisted the wisdom of her mother. Grace felt that she had lost her daughter; she could hardly recognize her as the same person.

She fretted for years, putting her name on every prayer list she could find. However, her daughter's life became even more destructive. She left college and moved in with her boyfriend. He abused her physically and emotionally, and eventually she had to enforce a restraining order on him.

During this period, she returned home for a short time, and Grace was shocked to see the change in her daughter. Grace fasted and prayed, but saw no results. Her daughter went back out on her own, and this time she got pregnant and gave birth to a little girl. She would go out to parties and sometimes not come home for a day or two, leaving her daughter with babysitters or with her mother.

Then Grace became aware of the power of decrees. She had been worrying about her daughter for years, but now decided to cast all her cares on the Lord and simply let His Word do the work. Every day through decrees, she sent forth His Word over her daughter and granddaughter. At first, she did not see any results. (In fact, her daughter's behavior became even more irresponsible.) But Grace did not lose faith. She trusted that the Lord would honor His Word and bring her daughter back into alignment with the truth and her destiny. She refused to be shaken by what she saw. Within two years of the first of these daily decrees, Grace's daughter had an encounter with God. The fire of His great love flooded her body, soul and spirit. In one single encounter she was transformed. In the months that followed, her life came into alignment and she was positioned for blessing. The family was healed.

Mark and Linda's Story

Mark and Linda had struggled financially from the moment they got married. They could not seem to make ends meet. Employment opportunities would come and go, and nothing stabilized for them. They were committed believers, but there seemed to be a warfare in their marriage in the area of provision. They were tithing, giving offerings and trying their best to steward what came into their hands. One day, they heard about the power of decrees and began to commit to making daily decrees to establish blessing in their home. Very quickly things turned around for them. They both received raises and promotions within the next few months, and the money just seemed to go further. They had furniture given to them, a new car and other blessings. Decrees had made all the difference. Peace and provision filled their home.

Decrees provide protection, favor, love and blessings for families. When a family lives under the banner of God's Word, they will experience His peace and harmony. Families are meant to live in a heavenly environment, and decrees will help you carve out that realm.

QUESTIONS TO PONDER

1. Why are strong family units so important to God—and so important to society?

2. What are some of the benefits individuals and families experience when we send forth the Word through decrees?

3. Read through both the following decree and the Scriptures on which it is based. Is your family (or are individual family members) living out some concerning "facts" (review chapter 2) where these biblical truths need to take over and become firmly established? Decree the entire decree, but highlight those points in particular; memorize them and continue to decree throughout the day, not only to establish the truth but as an encouragement and faith-builder.

Decree

Family and Children

As for me and my family, we will serve the Lord. Because I believe in the Lord Jesus Christ, I shall be saved, along with my entire household. Because I am a covenant child of God, my household is blessed. Blessings come upon us and overtake us.

My family, home, marriage and children are blessed, as is all that I put my hands to. I am blessed coming in and I am blessed going out. The Lord has established my household as a people for Himself. He causes us to abound in prosperity: the offspring of our bodies, the offspring of our animals and the produce of our property. The Lord surrounds my family and entire household with favor like a shield. No good thing does He withhold from us. His banner is love over my home, marriage and family. No weapon formed against us as a family prospers. What the Lord has blessed, no man can curse. We abide in the shadow of the Almighty and no evil befalls us.

My children shall be successful, even as signs and wonders for the world to see, because the homes of the upright are blessed.

My children will flourish like young olive plants as they sit around my table. My sons in their youth are like well-nurtured plants and my daughters as strong and graceful as pillars in a palace. They are a gift from the Lord—the fruit of the womb is my reward. I am like a warrior and my children are like arrows in my quiver.

Lord, Your covenant with me declares that Your Spirit that is upon me and Your words that You have put in my mouth shall not depart from my mouth, nor from the mouths of my children, nor from the mouths of my children's children. As all my children are taught of the Lord, their peace and prosperity will increase. They will be established in righteousness and kept far from oppression. They will not be led into temptation and they will know deliverance from evil.

My children are pure in heart, and therefore they shall see God. They hunger and thirst after righteousness; therefore they are filled. As the Spirit of the Lord is poured out upon my children, they prophesy. The Lord's blessing is upon them. They will grow up like well-watered saplings. One will say, "I am the Lord's," another will declare himself to be one of Jacob's descendants, while others will write on their hands: "Belonging to the Lord."

I declare that my children are seekers of wisdom and understanding. They hold fast to Your Word and to Your ways. They treasure Your commandments and they seek discernment. They (and their children, also) speak words of wisdom because the spirit of wisdom has been poured out so liberally upon our family.

The Lord will always keep my family from falling and, with great joy, He will present them blameless before the presence of the Father's glory.

Scripture references used in this decree

Joshua 24:15; Acts 16:31; Isaiah 59:21; Ephesians 1:3; Deuteronomy 28:1–12; Psalm 5:12; 84:11; Song of Solomon 2:4; Isaiah 54:17; Numbers 23:20; Psalm 91:1, 10; Psalm 112:2; Isaiah 8:18; Psalm 128:3; 127:3–4; 144:12; Joshua 1:8; Isaiah 54:13–14; Matthew 6:13; 5:6, 8; Acts 2:17; Isaiah 44:3–5; Proverbs 2:2–3; 1:23; Jude 24

sixteen

Empowered with Christ's Anointing

Believers are commissioned in Christ to "go into all the world and preach the gospel to every creature" (Mark 16:15 NKJV). Our mission as followers of Christ is to fill the earth with the knowledge of His glory.

From the moment I was born again, I had a passion to tell others about Jesus. I had not received any training in evangelism yet, but I followed my heart, sharing what I had experienced in God. As a result, by the grace of God, many came to Christ. In the years following, I received training in evangelism and led many teams to reach the lost. We also had the honor of establishing outreach centers in various places around the world. I discovered that prayer and, in particular, decrees of the Word, were vital parts of successful outreach. We never went out on the streets before we had prayed and decreed the Word.

I fondly remember one night back in the 1980s when I gathered a team of five believers together to accompany me on an outreach to the inner city of Vancouver, British Columbia, Canada. Three of the team had never been with us on an outreach before, so I was giving them instruction in prayer and evangelism as we traveled in our "hippie van" to our destination. We had an hour's drive ahead of us, so we prayed up a storm in the back of the van. We made decrees such as, "Lord, in Jesus' name we decree that we will have divine favor and supernatural connections with the lost tonight. We decree that we are empowered by the Holy Spirit to preach the Gospel and work miracles."

We continued to pray, decree and praise as we traveled. At one point, I lifted my head and looked out the window. A block ahead of us, I noticed a man hitchhiking. I felt prompted by the Spirit to have the driver stop the van and pick him up. He climbed into the van and immediately was faced with five Spirit-filled, fired-up "Jesus-lovers." The atmosphere of the van was filled with God's tangible presence, and in less than fifteen minutes he had come to know Jesus as his personal Savior. We proceeded to pray for him to be filled with the Spirit, and a demon manifested. Right there in the van, we cast the evil spirit out and then finished leading him into the baptism of the Spirit with the evidence of speaking in tongues. He asked if he could join us for the night rather than going to the party he had previously planned on attending.

He joined us on the streets that night, and we had the blessing of leading many to the Lord and praying for deliverances. Our new convert began his life in Christ witnessing God's love at work. He was never the same after that.

In 2001, our ministry hosted our first training in "prophetic evangelism."* Over a hundred and twenty students attended

---

*Prophetic evangelism involves using the gift of prophecy to minister to the lost. Through the prophetic gifting, God reveals destiny and insights for their lives. As a result, many come to Christ.

that initial training. Following the classroom instruction, we launched them into various outreaches using the prophetic gift. Before going out to the streets, we spent time in prayer and making decrees so that we would "go in the fullness of the blessing of the gospel of Christ" (Romans 15:29 NKJV). I also assigned a team of intercessors to pray and decree over the team on the streets the entire time they were engaged in the outreach.

About a dozen teams undertook various creative opportunities to reach the lost. We set up one group in a juice café in the midst of a tourist area with some New Age shops surrounding it. The owners allowed us to use five tables in their restaurant to host prophetic teams. We put a big sign out in front of the café announcing, "Free Spiritual Readings Today." We also passed out flyers inviting people to meet us at the juice café to receive their "spiritual reading." (We decided not to use the word "prophecy" in our marketing, as visitors would probably not understand the meaning of that word and we wanted to be relevant to the New Age demographic in the area.) When we opened the restaurant for the "spiritual readings," a long line of people wanted to receive a word, hungry for a word from God concerning their lives. Every team was busy hearing from God, and great grace and glory filled the place. Many received the Lord in the juice café that day, and many others were touched by God's tangible presence.

Every team reaching out in the city that day was successful— the favor of the Lord was on them! I truly believe it was the prayer covering that made the difference. Since that time, I have been committed to engaging in faith-filled prayer and decrees prior to going out on outreach, and often we also have intercessors covering the teams while they are out.

Every day, we all go somewhere. You might not go on a scheduled evangelism outreach, but you will probably go to a workplace, school, shopping mall, grocery store or activity within your neighborhood or community. As you go, remember that you have been commissioned to be a carrier of His light and power, releasing His love, glory and presence into the world you live in. This is normal Christianity.

When you are clothed in His Word, you are clothed in His light, love and power, and as a result you become an effective representative of Christ everywhere you go. *Decrees will clothe you in His Word, and then you can go forth with confidence!*

QUESTIONS TO PONDER

1. Does the thought of personal and street evangelism excite you, or does it put dread or fear in your soul? If it is the latter, taking into account everything you have learned regarding the power of decrees in this book, how can faith-filled prayers and decreeing the Word change both your perspective and your effectiveness?

2. Think about a typical day in your life. Where do you go? Who do you encounter? How often do you practice normal Christianity, carrying His light and power, releasing His love, glory and presence wherever you

go and to whomever you encounter? If it is very infrequently, what is deterring you?

_____

_____

_____

3. Read the decree that follows. Which aspects of this decree are (or are becoming) facts in your life, and which are still truths you have not yet attained to the fullest? Are you hungry for them to become truths in your life? What do you plan to do about it?

_____

_____

_____

Decree

Empowered with Christ's Anointing

I receive power when the Holy Spirit comes upon me to be the Lord's witness even to the uttermost parts of the earth. In Jesus' name I go into all the world to preach the Gospel to every creature.

These signs follow me as I go, because I believe: In the name of Jesus, I cast out devils, I speak with new tongues, I take up serpents, and if I drink any deadly poison it shall not harm me. When I lay hands on the sick, they shall recover. I go forth and preach everywhere, and the Lord confirms the Word I preach with signs that follow. When I go, I go in the fullness of the blessing of the Gospel of Christ.

171

The works that Jesus does, I do also in His name and even greater works I do because He has gone to the Father. Greater is He that is in me than he that is in the world. Jesus has given me power over all the power of the enemy. He has given me power ov,er unclean spirits to cast them out and has enabled me to heal all manner of sickness and all manner of disease.

As I go, I will preach, saying, "The Kingdom of heaven is at hand." I will heal the sick and raise the dead. I will cast out devils. I have received freely, so I will freely give. The Lord grants me boldness to speak His word. He stretches out His hand toward me to heal, that signs and wonders may be done through the name of Jesus Christ. His Spirit has been poured out upon me, and therefore I prophesy in His name.

All power in heaven and on earth has been given to Jesus Christ. I will go in His name and teach all nations, baptizing them in the name of the Father, the Son and the Holy Spirit. I will teach them to observe all things that Jesus has taught me. Jesus is with me even to the end of the world. He has called me to Himself and has given me power and authority over all devils and to cure diseases. He has sent me to preach the Kingdom of God and to heal the sick. As I go, Jesus prepares my way with His favor, for the Lord surrounds His righteous with favor like a shield. He sends His angels before me to watch over my ways and to bear me up, lest I fall.

Like Jesus, I have been anointed with the Holy Spirit and with power. I go about doing good and healing all who are oppressed by the devil, for God is with me. He has anointed me to preach the Gospel to the poor.

He has sent me to proclaim release to the captives and recovery of sight to the blind, to set free all who are downtrodden and to proclaim the favorable year of the Lord.

I arise and shine because my light has come, and the glory of the Lord has risen upon me. Although darkness shall cover the earth and its people, the Lord's glory appears upon me. People from many nations, even those who are in authority, will come to my light in Christ.

My speech and my preaching are not filled with enticing words of man's wisdom, but rather with the demonstration of the Spirit and of power, so that the faith of those I preach to will not be based on human wisdom but always on the power of God. The Kingdom of God is not in word only, but also in power.

According to His glorious riches and power, the Lord strengthens me with might by His Spirit in my inner man, bringing me through all adversities with patience and joy. I do all of my work in His power, which works mightily within me.

I do not preach about myself, but I always preach about Christ Jesus as Lord, with myself as a servant and messenger of Christ and His Body for Jesus' sake. For God, who said, "Light shall shine out of darkness," is the One who has shone in my heart to give the light of the knowledge of the glory of God in the face of Christ. I carry this treasure in the clay pot of my body, so that the surpassing greatness of the power of God will clearly be seen as His and not mine.

Now unto the King eternal, immortal, invisible, the only wise God who is able to do exceedingly, abundantly above all that I could ask or think according to the power that works within me, be honor and glory forever and ever.

Scripture references used in this decree

Acts 1:8; Mark 16:15–21; Romans 15:29; John 14:12; 1 John 4:4; Luke 10:19; Matthew 10:1, 7–8; Acts 4:29–30; 2:17; Matthew 28:18–20; Acts 10:38; Luke 9:2; Psalm 5:12; 91:11; Luke 4:18; Isaiah 60:1–3; 1 Corinthians 2:4; 4:20; Ephesians 3:16; Colossians 1:11, 29; 2 Corinthians 4:5–7; 1 Timothy 1:17; Ephesians 3:20

seventeen

Business, Workplace, Ministry

Most believers labor regularly in a place of business, a workplace or an outreach of Christian ministry. These are our arenas of influence in the world, and God wants us to be fruitful, successful and favored in these environments.

I have discovered that when individuals decree God's Word over their businesses, workplaces and ministries, blessings increase in multiple realms, including their finances, their ability to influence others and to fulfill their assignments, and in the distribution of their resources and message. I have personally regularly enjoyed numerous benefits that have come as a result of declaring daily decrees over these areas of my life.

The following are some testimonies of breakthrough from others:

Business

Charles and his wife Erin (not their real names) were struggling. They had taken a leap of faith to move to a new city and start a company. They had honorably resigned from their previous places of employment, taken their savings and with excitement launched into their dream.

They had a six-month buffer in their savings, and they were hoping to be financially established within that time. However, unforeseen circumstances had slowed things down. Their business did not take off as they had thought it would, and their finances were dwindling. In the face of difficult challenges, they were discouraged.

They became aware of the power of Word decrees and added them to their daily prayer time. They were faithful every morning to decree the Word, and when they did not have clients in their shop, they decreed the blessings of the Word of God over their business and their life. They took every opportunity to establish God's Word in the heart of their business.

Within three months, things turned around. Over the coming years, their business became established in their community and God blessed them greatly. Decrees made the difference.

Workplace

A mother was training her son to enter the work world through a part-time job at a pizza restaurant. He was only sixteen years old, and he had never held a job previously. He was slated to work on weekends and after school. However, his first day on the job was overwhelming for him. That night happened to be very busy and chaotic, and he made many mistakes. His boss was visibly impatient with him while he struggled to absorb all that he was expected to accomplish. When he finished his shift, his mother picked him up and asked him how he made out—and he fought to hold back the tears.

He felt like a failure, and he did not want to go back. In fact, he wanted to quit. His mother encouraged him and pulled out some decrees for him to declare over his life. They decreed them together a couple of times on the spot, and then she had him decree them on his own. That night he went to bed with hope.

The next time he went to work, he decreed the Word over his life before he left his house. He was delightfully surprised to find that night was quite different from his first; everything fell into place for him. He ended up winning the Employee of the Month award in his third month of employment. He is sold on decrees!

Ministry

Often people who are called into ministry are required to resign from their places of employment, believe for financial support and leave family and friends in order to pursue the call. The initial season of engagement can be very taxing. It certainly was for Joe and Tina, a young married couple from a midwestern state who felt called to be "prayer missionaries" in another nation that they carried a burden for. Along with raising some financial support to sustain their essential daily needs, they used their savings to register for the mandatory yearlong training program, and they diligently studied the language of the people. They loved the training period and enjoyed learning the language, although they missed their families and fought waves of homesickness.

When they finished their training, they were assigned by their leaders to oversee a prayer center in the heart of an inner city in that nation. Seven other team members were also assigned to this post to help them in their mission. Joe and Tina were excited about the assignment, as were the other members of their team, and they labored with zeal as they prayed for the transformation of the area. The center was very small and humble, but it was at least a start. Situated in a neighborhood where there was much corruption, theft, drug-dealing and pimping, the team at the center was a light for God, invading a very dark environment.

They had not been at their post for even two weeks before all hell broke loose against them. They had begun by establishing a daily schedule of prayer in two shifts: from 5:00 a.m. until noon and from 5:00 p.m. until midnight. Early one morning they entered the prayer room for their session, only to discover that the center had been broken into and all the sound equipment and musical instruments were stolen. On that same day, the mother of one of their team members was diagnosed with an inoperable tumor, and the team member had to leave immediately to care for her mother. Then two other team members began to dispute with each other, which caused an atmosphere of contention and division among the four remaining members of their team. To top it all off, one of the pimps and drug dealers in the area stopped by the center and threatened their lives. The following week they discovered that one of their most committed financial supporters needed to withdraw support, leaving them with very little to cover their essentials.

They were overwhelmed by the assaults but did not lose hope, even though the more they prayed, the worse things seemed to get. They persisted. A friend back in their hometown was aware of their situation and had been praying. She had recently been introduced to teaching on the power of the decree. She sent them a sheet of decrees to declare over their lives and ministry and encouraged them to proclaim them numerous times a day. She also alerted some people on her prayer team and emailed them the decrees to declare over this couple, their team and their assignment.

Within two months of making the focused decrees, things started to turn. Miracle provision came in the form of a gift of a better sound system than they had previously used, and one by one the musical instruments were replaced. Personal finances as well as ministry finances began to pour in. Peace and love overflowed in the team. Best of all, local people started coming to Jesus, including the pimp/drug dealer who had threatened them earlier.

This was amazing. The power of decrees had turned everything around!

Remember, the Word of God does not return void but accomplishes everything it has been sent to do. *Diligently decree the Word over your business, workplace and ministry and see what God will do.*

QUESTIONS TO PONDER

1. What is God's desire for us in regard to our businesses, workplaces and ministries? Do you feel that you have fulfilled both His and your desires in regard to these? Why or why not?

2. How are you influencing others through your business, workplace or ministry, whether it be those in your immediate surroundings or as far-reaching as your city or other nations?

3. What are some of the multiple realms of blessing that can be experienced as a result of decreeing the Word? Which of these realms of blessing would you like to see more of in your own business, workplace or ministry?

Decrees

Business, Workplace, Ministry

In my business, workplace and ministry, I am surrounded with favor as a shield. The Lord commands blessings upon me so that my every project and assignment prospers and bears fruit. He establishes my business, workplace and ministry as holy.

I arise and shine, for my Light has come, and I carry His glory wherever I go, so that people can see it. As long as I walk in obedience to the Lord, I am the head and not the tail. I am always above, not beneath.

Because I am in Christ, I show no defect but always function in intelligence in every branch of wisdom, being endowed with understanding, discernment, knowledge and inventiveness. The Lord causes me to grow in wisdom, in stature and in favor with God and man.

The blessing of the Lord makes my business, workplace and ministry rich in every aspect of life; He provides everything I need, without sorrow, and wealthy people seek my favor.

I do not submit my business, workplace and ministry to the world system, but instead to the Kingdom of God and His righteousness. The integrity of the Lord guides me in my affairs. The Lord looks favorably upon me and makes everything I put my hand to productive, causing it to multiply.

No weapon formed against my business, workplace or ministry prospers. Every tongue that rises up against it in judgment I condemn to silence, and the Lord vindicates me. The Lord is a wall of fire around my business, workplace and ministry, and His glory is in the midst of it.

The Lord leads me by His presence, and He gives me rest. He brings goodness to pass within my business, workplace and ministry. His goodness and mercy follow me all the days of my life. Peace, unity, love, integrity, honor and servanthood are godly values that prevail in my business, workplace and ministry.

I decree that Jesus Christ is Lord over my life, business, workplace and ministry!

Scripture references used in this decree

Psalm 5:12; 133:3; 1:3; Deuteronomy 28:9; Isaiah 60:1–3; Deuteronomy 28:13; Colossians 1:22; 2 Chronicles 2:13; Proverbs 8:12; Luke 2:52; Proverbs 10:22; Psalm 45:12; Daniel 1:4; Matthew 6:33; Proverbs 11:3; Leviticus 26:9; Isaiah 54:17; Zechariah 2:5; Exodus 33:14, 19; Psalm 23:6

eighteen

Nations

God loves the nations of the earth! Each one is unique and will bring forth precious fruit before the Lord, according to the grace He has poured out upon it. Every nation is loaded with potential, and believers are to steward the purposes of God within and among the nations. Jesus said,

> "All authority has been given to Me in heaven and on earth. Go therefore and make disciples of all the nations, baptizing them in the name of the Father and the Son and the Holy Spirit, teaching them to observe all that I commanded you; and lo, I am with you always, even to the end of the age."
>
> Matthew 28:18–20

If the church does not disciple the nations, they will not fulfill their destinies. It is our mandate as believers to care for, nurture and teach the nations.

In the Word, we see that "nations, tribes and tongues" will stand before the throne (see Revelation 7:9). We also see that the nations will be judged (see Matthew 25:31–33). *Most of us think our mandate is to disciple individuals, but we have been assigned to nations as well; decrees are powerful tools when we stand in prayer before God on behalf of nations.*

Here is how it works. When our ministry first began serving in the nation of Cambodia, it was a war-torn nation recovering from a massive genocide. The nation had suffered under the Khmer Rouge regime, which was a cruel dictatorship under which literally masses of people had been killed, especially intellectuals, career professionals and the rich. The regime killed men, women and children without mercy. Entire villages were wiped out by the Khmer Rouge.

The nation was left in ruin, with only the poor, uneducated and the subservient remaining, for the most part. When the Khmer Rouge was finally brought down, the nation needed to build back up from the ground level. Sex traffickers, drug cartels, corrupt business owners and government leaders moved in, looking to take advantage of the people's ignorance and desperation.

One of our greatest initial tools in the beginning of our ministry in Cambodia was the use of Word decrees. We decreed them over the many faithful ministers and missionaries who had been laboring in the land for years, over the government leaders, the economy, villages and people. In spirit, we sent forth the Word to build a framework that the Spirit of God would honor and fill.

Now, with the significant help of godly decrees, the nation has been transformed to an amazing degree.

God has put a nation or nations on your heart. It could be the nation in which you reside or a nation that He has given you a love-burden for. You can send decrees into that nation, and they can bring change. I think of Esther, who was a deliverer for her nation in the face of the enemy's assignment to completely destroy her people. God powerfully intervened after Esther issued a decree in the name of the king. The decree settled the issue, and it caused the nation to be delivered and to flourish.

> Now you write to the Jews as you see fit, in the king's name, and seal it with the king's signet ring; for a decree which is written in the name of the king and sealed with the king's signet ring may not be revoked.
>
> Esther 8:8

In the same way, you can make a decree in the name of your king, King Jesus. Even one person in agreement with God's Word can potentially turn a nation to God.

QUESTIONS TO PONDER

1. Ponder the full meaning of what we know as the Great Commission—Matthew 28:18–20. What do you consider to be your part in its fulfillment? How about your church's part, and the role of the other ministries you are involved with? How can you partner with them?

2. Think about the nation you live in now. What are some concerning facts about it (see chapter 2) that need to

change? What are some eternal biblical truths you can decree over it?

_____

_____

_____

3. Has the Lord placed one or more nations on your heart? Perhaps these are nations you have visited, or perhaps you have partnered with others who are involved there. Perhaps mostly it is a prayer burden. What are some concerning facts about that nation (see chapter 2) that need to change? What are some eternal biblical truths you can decree over it?

_____

_____

_____

_____

Decrees

Nations

1. In Jesus' name, I decree that my nation is turning to God and is embracing the truth of His Word.
2. In Jesus' name, I decree that the active, holy and powerful conviction of the Holy Spirit is visiting every individual in my nation, drawing souls into true encounter with Christ.
3. In Jesus' name, I decree that all who serve my nation in government positions are being visited by the righteousness,

truth and justice of God, and that they live in the fullness of Christ's wisdom in all they do. I decree that any corruption in government will be exposed and dealt with in wisdom and righteousness in order for the nation to be cleansed.

4. In Jesus' name, I decree that the education leaders, systems and institutions in my nation are being filled with Kingdom values, wisdom, conviction and truth.

5. In Jesus' name, I decree that the Body of Christ in my nation is actively walking with and serving the Lord with fullness of focus, sincerity of faith and in the demonstration of the power of the Spirit.

6. In Jesus' name, I decree that those who live in my nation are being kept in good health and offered excellent health services. I decree that all are living in the health and strength of the Lord.

7. In Jesus' name, I decree that the media in my nation will communicate godly morals and values, and that the Gospel will be favored in media.

8. In Jesus' name, I decree that every godly business and enterprise will flourish in my nation and every corrupt business and enterprise will be exposed and fall. In my nation, I decree prosperity and fruitfulness as a result of godliness, in order for every individual to have all they need.

9. In Jesus' name, I decree that the marriages and families in my nation will be blessed with love, joy and peace and that every home is filled with the goodness of God.

10. In Jesus' name, I decree that the Body of Christ be mobilized into the harvest fields of my nation to bring forth much fruit.

11. In Jesus' name, I decree that righteousness thrives in my nation in every realm of life and that lawlessness and corruption have no place.

12. I decree that *Jesus is Lord over my nation!*

Scripture references used in this decree

John 14:13–14; Psalm 2:8; Luke 10:2; Genesis 1:28; 1 Timothy 2:2; 1 John 5:14–15; Mark 11:23–24

A Note from the Author

Dear Reader,

It has been my delight to share with you a subject for which I have great passion. Of all the equipping tools for a God-filled life that I have used in my personal walk with the Lord, decrees are by far my most favorite and the most effective.

I pray that the deep conviction and joy that I have for decrees has been imparted to you as you have read this book, and that as you regularly proclaim decrees of God's Word, you will see transformation, breakthrough and established blessing in your life. After all, if God said it, you can believe it. And that settles it!

May you be filled to overflowing with His love, His Word and His Spirit.

With delight, I decree this over you in His glorious name!

Patricia King

Patricia King has dedicated her life to inspiring and equipping believers to walk in their God-given callings. An apostolic and prophetic minister of the Gospel, she is also a successful business owner and an accomplished itinerant speaker, a seasoned television host and media producer, the author of many books and resources, and a capable ministry network overseer. She is a skilled communicator and gifted life coach. She is the founder of Patricia King Ministries and the Women in Ministry Network, and the co-founder of XPMedia.com.

She and her husband, Ron, live in Maricopa, Arizona. They have two adult sons and three grandchildren.

FOR MORE INFORMATION

PatriciaKing.com
patriciakingministries.com
XPmedia.com

More from Patricia King

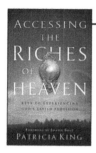

During seasons of hardship or shortage, we yearn for the peace and abundance we know we will find in heaven. But all of heaven's riches have your name on them, and you can access them here and now. Patricia King shares the keys, through the lens of Scripture, that will unlock your spiritual inheritance today.

Accessing the Riches of Heaven